HEMOCHROMATOSIS COOKBOOK

Featuring a 4-Week Cleanse, Budget-Friendly Meals, and Secrets for Optimal Health

AMBER T. KENNEDY

Copyright © 2024 By AMBER T. KENNEDY. All rights reserved worldwide.

No part of this book may be reproduced or transmitted in any form or by any means, electronic or mechanical, including photocopying, recording, or by any information storage and retrieval system, without written permission from the publisher, except for the inclusion of brief quotations in a review.

Warning-Disclaimer:

The purpose of this book is to educate and entertain. The author or publisher does not guarantee that anyone following the techniques, suggestions, tips, ideas, or strategies will become successful. The author and publisher shall have neither liability nor responsibility to anyone with respect to any loss or damage caused, or alleged to be caused, directly or indirectly, by the information contained in this book.

This copyright notice and disclaimer apply to the entirety of the book and its contents, whether in print or electronic form, and extend to all future editions or revisions of the book. Unauthorized use or reproduction of this book or its contents is strictly prohibited and may result in legal action.

TABLE OF CONTENTS

INTRODUCTION TO HEMOCHROMATOSIS 7

WHAT IS HEMOCHROMATOSIS? 9

UNDERSTANDING IRON OVERLOAD 11

BENEFITS OF A LOW-IRON DIET 13

TIPS FOR MEAL PLANNING AND PREPARATION 14

BREAKFAST OPTIONS 16

   Fruity Oatmeal Delight 16

   Herby Avocado Toast 16

   Berry Blast Smoothie Bowl 17

   Coconut Cinnamon Quinoa Porridge 17

   Spinach Bell Pepper Frittata Bites 18

   Mushroom Onion Tofu Scramble 19

   Berrylicious Chia Pudding Parfait 19

   Nutty Banana Toast 20

   Yogurt Fruit Salad Bowl 21

   Savory Sweet Potato Hash 21

   Apple Cinnamon Overnight Oats 22

   Nutty Zucchini Bread 23

   Vegan Pancakes with Maple Syrup 24

   Plant-Powered Breakfast Burrito 24

   Acai Bowl with Granola 25

SALADS AND APPETIZERS 27

   Beet, Orange, and Walnut Salad 27

   Quinoa Salad with Roasted Vegetables and Avocado 27

   Caprese Salad with Tomato, Mozzarella, and Basil 28

   Cucumber and Tomato Salad with Lemon Dressing 28

   Black Bean and Corn Salad with Cilantro Lime Dressing 29

   Hummus with Raw Vegetables and Pita Bread 30

   Guacamole with Baked Tortilla Chips 30

Roasted Vegetable Skewers with Balsamic Glaze 31

Watermelon and Feta Salad with Mint 32

Lentil and Roasted Vegetable Salad 32

Spinach and Strawberry Salad with Poppy Seed Dressing 33

Mediterranean Chickpea Salad with Olives and Feta 33

Avocado and Grapefruit Salad with Lime Vinaigrette 34

Grilled Peach and Arugula Salad with Balsamic Reduction 34

Vegetable Spring Rolls with Peanut Dipping Sauce...35

SOUPS AND STEWS 37

Vegetable Minestrone Soup...37

Lentil and Sweet Potato Stew 37

Tomato Basil Soup with Grilled Cheese Croutons...38

Vegan Chili with Avocado and Cilantro...39

Butternut Squash and Apple Soup 40

White Bean and Kale Soup... 41

Cauliflower and Potato Soup with Crispy Chickpeas 42

Vegetable Noodle Soup with Plant-Based Meatballs..43

Black Bean and Quinoa Chili 44

Roasted Red Pepper and Tomato Soup with Basil..45

Creamy Vegetable Soup with Cashew Cream.. 46

Split Pea and Vegetable Soup 46

Vegan Corn Chowder with Smoky Tempeh Bacon..47

Carrot and Ginger Soup with Coconut Milk 48

Vegetable and Tofu Miso Soup 49

MAIN DISHES: GRAINS, LEGUMES, AND VEGETABLES 50

Quinoa and Roasted Vegetable Bowls 50

Lentil and Vegetable Curry with Coconut Milk... 50

Baked Sweet Potatoes with Black Bean Chili 51

Whole Grain Pasta with Marinara Sauce and Roasted Veggies 52

Vegetable Stir-Fry with Brown Rice or Quinoa...53

Stuffed Bell Peppers with Rice and Plant-Based Protein 54

Vegetable and Tofu Pad Thai with Rice Noodles 55

Lentil and Vegetable Shepherd's Pie 56

Veggie Burgers with Sweet Potato Fries..57

Baked Falafel with Tahini Sauce and Salad..58

Grilled Portobello Mushroom Caps with Quinoa and Roasted Vegetables 59

Vegetable and Tofu Stir-Fry with Rice Noodles 60

Black Bean and Sweet Potato Enchiladas..61

Cauliflower and Chickpea Curry with Basmati Rice...62

Vegetable Lasagna with Plant-Based Cheese...63

MAIN DISHES: PLANT-BASED PROTEINS 65

Tofu Stir-Fry with Broccoli and Cashews..65

Lentil and Vegetable Meatballs with Marinara Sauce 66

Grilled Tempeh Kebabs with Pineapple and Bell Peppers..67

Chickpea and Spinach Curry with Coconut Milk 68

Vegetable and Tofu Stir-Fry with Peanut Sauce 69

Baked Tofu with Teriyaki Glaze and Steamed Vegetables..70

Lentil and Walnut Loaf with Mushroom Gravy 70

Seitan Fajitas with Grilled Vegetables and Guacamole 72

Tempeh and Vegetable Stir-Fry with Brown Rice 73

Chickpea and Vegetable Burgers with Sweet Potato Fries...74

Tofu and Vegetable Sushi Rolls with Pickled Ginger 75

Tempeh and Vegetable Fried Rice 76

Baked Seitan with BBQ Sauce and Roasted Vegetables 77

Chickpea and Spinach Stew with Whole Grain Pita...78

Tofu and Vegetable Pad Thai with Rice Noodles 79

SNACKS AND SIDES 81

Roasted Chickpeas with Spices... 81

Baked Sweet Potato Fries with Avocado Dipping Sauce 81

Kale Chips with Nutritional Yeast...82

Hummus and Veggie Wraps with Whole Grain Tortillas... 83

Avocado Toast with Tomato and Basil 83

Edamame with Sea Salt 84

Fruit Skewers with Yogurt Dipping Sauce 84

Baked Apple Chips with Cinnamon 85

Veggie and Tofu Spring Rolls with Peanut Dipping Sauce 86

Cucumber and Carrot Sticks with Tzatziki Sauce 87
Roasted Beet and Orange Salad with Walnuts 87
Quinoa and Black Bean Stuffed Avocados 88
Baked Zucchini Fries with Marinara Sauce 89
Roasted Cauliflower with Tahini Sauce 89
Grilled Pineapple with Coconut Yogurt Dip 90

SMOOTHIES AND JUICES 92

Green Smoothie with Spinach, Banana, and Plant-Based Milk 92
Berry and Nut Smoothie with Chia Seeds 92
Tropical Smoothie with Mango, Pineapple, and Coconut Milk 93
Vegetable and Fruit Juice with Ginger and Turmeric 93
Chocolate and Avocado Smoothie with Plant-Based Milk 94
Carrot and Orange Juice with Ginger 94
Peanut Butter and Banana Smoothie with Oats 95
Blueberry and Kale Smoothie with Almond Milk 95
Mango and Spinach Smoothie with Plant-Based Yogurt 96
Strawberry and Beet Smoothie with Coconut Water 96
Pineapple and Mint Smoothie with Plant-Based Milk 97
Green Juice with Cucumber, Celery, and Apple 97
Chocolate and Peanut Butter Smoothie with Plant-Based Protein Powder 98
Tropical Green Smoothie with Spinach, Mango, and Coconut Milk 99
Watermelon and Lime Juice with Mint 99

BAKED GOODS AND DESSERTS 100

Vegan Banana Bread with Walnuts 100
Oatmeal and Apple Baked Crisp with Cinnamon 101
Chocolate Avocado Pudding with Coconut Whipped Cream 101
Fruit and Nut Granola Bars 102
Baked Apples with Cinnamon and Raisins 103
Vegan Pumpkin Bread with Pecan Streusel 104
Chocolate and Almond Butter Energy Bites 105
Lemon and Blueberry Muffins 106
Vegan Carrot Cake with Cashew Cream Frosting 107
Baked Pears with Honey and Walnuts 108

Coconut and Dark Chocolate Truffles ... 109
Oatmeal and Raisin Cookies ... 110
Vegan Brownies with Walnuts ... 111
Baked Peaches with Maple and Cinnamon ... 111
Coconut and Berry Chia Pudding Parfaits ... 112

BEVERAGES AND CONDIMENTS ... 114

Herbal Teas ... 114
Nut and Plant-Based Milk (Almond Milk) ... 114
Fresh Fruit-Infused Water ... 115
Homemade Nut Butter (Peanut Butter) ... 115
Vegetable and Herb Pesto ... 115
Roasted Chickpeas with Spices ... 116
Baked Sweet Potato Fries with Avocado Dipping Sauce ... 117
Kale Chips with Nutritional Yeast ... 117
Hummus and Veggie Wraps with Whole Grain Tortillas ... 118
Roasted Beet and Orange Salad with Walnuts ... 118
Quinoa and Black Bean Stuffed Avocados ... 119
Baked Zucchini Fries with Marinara Sauce ... 120
Roasted Cauliflower with Tahini Sauce ... 120
Tofu Stir-Fry with Broccoli and Cashews ... 121
Lentil and Vegetable Meatballs with Marinara Sauce ... 122

CONCLUSION ... 123

INTRODUCTION TO HEMOCHROMATOSIS

Hemochromatosis is a genetic disorder characterized by excessive absorption of dietary iron by the body. This condition leads to the accumulation of iron in various organs, including the liver, heart, pancreas, and joints, which can cause serious health complications if left untreated. Hemochromatosis is often referred to as an "iron overload" disorder, as the body absorbs more iron than it needs and cannot effectively excrete the excess.

While hemochromatosis is primarily caused by genetic mutations, certain dietary and lifestyle factors can exacerbate the condition. Consuming foods rich in iron, such as red meat, liver, fortified cereals, and iron supplements, can significantly increase iron levels in the body. For individuals with hemochromatosis, managing their iron intake through a low-iron diet is crucial to prevent further iron accumulation and reduce the risk of complications.

A low-iron diet aims to restrict the consumption of foods that are high in iron, while still providing essential nutrients for overall health and well-being. This dietary approach focuses on selecting foods that are naturally low in iron or processed to remove iron content. It emphasizes the importance of balance and moderation in food choices, while also considering individual preferences and cultural practices.

Key components of a low-iron diet include limiting or avoiding red meat, organ meats, shellfish, iron-fortified foods, and vitamin C supplements, as vitamin C enhances iron absorption. Instead, individuals are encouraged to consume a variety of fruits, vegetables, whole grains, legumes, nuts, seeds, and lean proteins with lower iron content. These foods not only help regulate iron levels but also provide essential vitamins, minerals, antioxidants, and fiber that support overall health.

In addition to dietary modifications, individuals with hemochromatosis may benefit from other lifestyle changes to manage their condition effectively. These may include regular blood donations to reduce iron levels, avoiding alcohol consumption, maintaining a healthy weight, staying physically active, and working closely with healthcare professionals to monitor iron levels and adjust treatment as needed.

It's important to note that while a low-iron diet can help manage hemochromatosis, it should be personalized to meet individual needs and preferences. Consulting with a registered dietitian or healthcare provider who specializes in hemochromatosis management is recommended to develop a comprehensive dietary plan tailored to specific goals and health considerations.

By adopting a low-iron diet and making lifestyle adjustments, individuals with hemochromatosis can take proactive steps to manage their condition, reduce the risk of complications, and improve overall quality of life. This cookbook aims to provide practical guidance, delicious recipes, and nutritional information to support individuals on their journey to better health and well-being despite the challenges of hemochromatosis.

WHAT IS HEMOCHROMATOSIS?

Hemochromatosis is a hereditary disorder characterized by excessive absorption of dietary iron by the body. This condition leads to the accumulation of iron in various organs, including the liver, heart, pancreas, and joints, which can cause serious health complications if left untreated. Hemochromatosis is primarily caused by mutations in genes involved in regulating iron absorption, most commonly the HFE gene.

The body typically absorbs iron from food and releases it as needed to maintain healthy levels. However, in individuals with hemochromatosis, this regulation mechanism is disrupted, leading to the continuous absorption of iron even when the body has sufficient stores. As a result, excess iron accumulates in tissues and organs over time, causing damage and impairing their normal functions.

The symptoms of hemochromatosis vary widely among affected individuals and can range from mild to severe. Early signs and symptoms may include fatigue, joint pain, abdominal pain, weakness, and loss of libido. As iron levels continue to rise, more serious complications may develop, such as liver cirrhosis, diabetes, heart problems, arthritis, and an increased risk of certain cancers.

Hemochromatosis is often referred to as an "iron overload" disorder because of the excessive accumulation of iron in the body tissues. It is one of the most common genetic disorders in people of European descent, particularly those of Northern European ancestry. However, it can occur in individuals of any ethnic background.

Diagnosis of hemochromatosis typically involves a combination of medical history assessment, physical examination, blood tests to measure iron levels and assess organ function, and genetic testing to identify mutations associated with the disorder. Early detection and intervention are essential to prevent or minimize the long-term complications of hemochromatosis.

Treatment for hemochromatosis focuses on reducing iron levels in the body to normal or near-normal levels and preventing further iron accumulation. This may involve therapeutic phlebotomy, a procedure similar to blood donation, to remove excess iron from the body. In some cases, iron-chelating medications may be prescribed to help remove excess iron from the body.

In addition to medical treatment, lifestyle modifications such as adopting a low-iron diet, avoiding iron supplements, limiting alcohol consumption, and maintaining a healthy weight are important components of managing hemochromatosis. Regular monitoring of iron levels and organ function is also crucial to assess treatment effectiveness and adjust management strategies as needed.

Overall, hemochromatosis is a complex genetic disorder characterized by excessive iron absorption and accumulation in the body, leading to a wide range of symptoms and complications. Early diagnosis, treatment, and lifestyle modifications can help individuals with hemochromatosis manage their condition effectively and minimize its impact on their health and quality of life.

UNDERSTANDING IRON OVERLOAD

Iron overload, also known as hemochromatosis, is a condition characterized by excessive accumulation of iron in the body. Iron is an essential mineral that plays a vital role in various physiological processes, including oxygen transport, energy production, and DNA synthesis. However, when the body absorbs more iron than it needs or can effectively utilize, the excess iron accumulates in tissues and organs, leading to damage and dysfunction.

The primary cause of iron overload is genetic mutations that disrupt the normal regulation of iron absorption and metabolism. The most common form of hereditary hemochromatosis is caused by mutations in the HFE gene, which regulates the absorption of dietary iron in the intestines. Other less common forms of hemochromatosis are caused by mutations in genes involved in iron transport, storage, or utilization.

In addition to hereditary factors, secondary causes of iron overload may include frequent blood transfusions, certain types of anemia, liver disease, or excessive iron supplementation. These factors can disrupt the body's normal iron balance and lead to increased iron accumulation over time.

The symptoms of iron overload can vary widely among affected individuals and may depend on the severity of the condition and the organs affected. Early symptoms may include fatigue, joint pain, abdominal pain, weakness, and loss of libido. As iron levels continue to rise, more serious complications may develop, such as liver cirrhosis, diabetes, heart problems, arthritis, and an increased risk of certain cancers.

Diagnosing iron overload typically involves a combination of medical history assessment, physical examination, blood tests to measure iron levels and assess organ function, and genetic testing to identify mutations associated with hereditary hemochromatosis. Early detection is crucial to prevent or minimize the long-term complications of iron overload.

Treatment for iron overload aims to reduce iron levels in the body to normal or near-normal levels and prevent further iron accumulation. Therapeutic phlebotomy, a procedure similar to blood donation, is often used to remove excess iron from the body. In some cases, iron-chelating medications may be prescribed to help remove excess iron from the body.

In addition to medical treatment, lifestyle modifications such as adopting a low-iron diet, avoiding iron supplements, limiting alcohol consumption, and maintaining a healthy weight are important components of managing iron overload. Regular monitoring of iron levels and organ function is also crucial to assess treatment effectiveness and adjust management strategies as needed.

Overall, iron overload is a complex condition characterized by excessive accumulation of iron in the body, leading to a wide range of symptoms and complications. Early diagnosis, treatment, and lifestyle modifications can help individuals with iron overload manage their condition effectively and minimize its impact on their health and quality of life.

BENEFITS OF A LOW-IRON DIET

A low-iron diet offers numerous benefits for individuals with conditions such as hemochromatosis, iron overload, or those needing to reduce iron intake for various health reasons. Firstly, it helps to regulate iron levels in the body, preventing excessive accumulation that can lead to organ damage and complications. By restricting foods high in iron, individuals can better manage their condition and reduce the risk of associated health problems.

Secondly, a low-iron diet promotes overall health and well-being by encouraging the consumption of a diverse range of nutrient-rich foods. While some high-iron foods are restricted, individuals are encouraged to include plenty of fruits, vegetables, whole grains, legumes, nuts, and seeds in their diet. These foods provide essential vitamins, minerals, antioxidants, and fiber that support optimal health and contribute to a balanced diet.

Moreover, a low-iron diet can help alleviate symptoms associated with iron overload, such as fatigue, joint pain, and abdominal discomfort. By reducing iron intake and avoiding foods that exacerbate the condition, individuals may experience improvements in their quality of life and overall sense of well-being.

Additionally, adopting a low-iron diet can support the effectiveness of medical treatments for iron overload, such as therapeutic phlebotomy or iron-chelating medications. By complementing these treatments with dietary modifications, individuals can enhance their management of iron overload and improve treatment outcomes.

Furthermore, a low-iron diet promotes awareness of dietary choices and encourages mindful eating habits. Individuals learn to read food labels, identify high-iron foods, and make informed decisions about their dietary intake. This increased awareness can empower individuals to take control of their health and make positive lifestyle changes.

Lastly, a low-iron diet can be beneficial for individuals with certain medical conditions or dietary preferences that require reduced iron intake. For example, individuals with certain types of anemia, chronic kidney disease, or inflammatory bowel disease may benefit from limiting their iron intake to prevent complications or alleviate symptoms.

In conclusion, a low-iron diet offers a range of benefits for individuals with conditions requiring reduced iron intake. By regulating iron levels, promoting overall health, alleviating symptoms, supporting medical treatments, fostering mindful eating habits, and accommodating specific dietary needs, a low-iron diet plays a vital role in managing iron overload and optimizing health and well-being.

TIPS FOR MEAL PLANNING AND PREPARATION

Meal planning and preparation are essential for successfully implementing a low-iron diet and managing conditions such as hemochromatosis or iron overload. Here are some tips to help make meal planning and preparation easier and more effective:

1. Educate Yourself: Learn about foods that are high and low in iron to make informed choices when planning meals. Familiarize yourself with alternative sources of protein, such as beans, lentils, tofu, and seafood with lower iron content.

2. Plan Ahead: Take time to plan your meals for the week, considering your dietary restrictions and preferences. Choose recipes that are low in iron and incorporate a variety of nutrient-rich foods to ensure a balanced diet.

3. Create a Grocery List: Based on your meal plan, create a grocery list of ingredients you'll need for the week. Stick to your list while shopping to avoid purchasing high-iron foods that may tempt you.

4. Stock Up on Staples: Keep your pantry stocked with staple ingredients for low-iron cooking, such as whole grains, legumes, canned tomatoes, herbs, and spices. Having these items on hand makes it easier to throw together quick and nutritious meals.

5. Batch Cook: Set aside time each week to batch cook large quantities of staple foods like grains, beans, and vegetables. This makes meal preparation during the week much quicker and reduces the temptation to opt for convenience foods that may not align with your dietary needs.

6. Embrace Variety: Experiment with different cuisines and cooking techniques to keep your meals interesting and flavorful. Incorporate a variety of fruits, vegetables, herbs, and spices to add depth and complexity to your dishes.

7. Plan for Leftovers: Cook extra portions of meals to have leftovers for future meals or lunches. This saves time and ensures that you always have nutritious options on hand when you're short on time.

8. Use Kitchen Tools: Invest in kitchen tools and appliances that make meal preparation easier, such as a slow cooker, Instant Pot, food processor, or blender. These tools can help you whip up delicious and nutritious meals with minimal effort.

9. Stay Organized: Keep your kitchen organized and clutter-free to streamline meal preparation. Store ingredients in clear containers, label them for easy identification, and arrange your kitchen tools and utensils in a way that makes cooking efficient.

10. Be Flexible: Don't be afraid to adjust your meal plan and recipes based on what's available at the grocery store or your dietary preferences. Flexibility is key to successful meal planning and ensures that you can adapt to changing circumstances without sacrificing nutrition or taste.

By following these tips for meal planning and preparation, you can simplify the process of adhering to a low-iron diet and make it easier to manage your condition effectively while enjoying delicious and nutritious meals.

BREAKFAST OPTIONS

Fruity Oatmeal Delight

Prep: 5 mins | Cook: 10 mins | Serves: 2

Ingredients:

- 1 cup rolled oats (US) / 100g rolled oats (UK)
- 2 cups water or plant-based milk (US) / 500ml water or plant-based milk (UK)
- 1 banana, sliced
- 1/2 cup mixed berries (US) / 75g mixed berries (UK)
- 2 tbsp chopped nuts (US) / 30g chopped nuts (UK)

Instructions:

1. In a saucepan, bring the water or plant-based milk to a gentle boil.
2. Stir in the rolled oats and reduce heat to low. Simmer for about 5-7 minutes, stirring occasionally, until the oats are cooked and the mixture thickens.
3. Remove from heat and divide the oatmeal into serving bowls.
4. Top each bowl with sliced banana, mixed berries, and chopped nuts.
5. Serve hot and enjoy this nutritious breakfast option!

Nutritional Info (per serving): Calories: 25 Fat: 6g Carbs: 42g Protein: 7g

Herby Avocado Toast

Prep: 5 mins | Cook: 5 mins | Serves: 2

Ingredients:

- 2 slices whole grain bread (US) / 2 slices wholemeal bread (UK)
- 1 ripe avocado
- 1 small tomato, sliced
- Fresh herbs (such as parsley or cilantro), chopped
- Salt and pepper to taste

Instructions:

1. Toast the slices of bread until golden brown and crispy.
2. While the bread is toasting, mash the ripe avocado in a bowl with a fork until smooth.
3. Spread the mashed avocado evenly onto the toasted bread slices.
4. Top each slice with tomato slices and a sprinkle of fresh chopped herbs.
5. Season with salt and pepper to taste.

6. Serve immediately for a delicious and satisfying breakfast!

Nutritional Info (per serving): Calories: 220 Fat: 10g Carbs: 26g Protein: 6g

Berry Blast Smoothie Bowl

Prep: 5 mins | Serves: 1

Ingredients:

- 1 cup mixed frozen berries (US) / 150g mixed frozen berries (UK)
- 1 ripe banana, frozen
- 1/2 cup almond milk or other plant-based milk (US) / 125ml almond milk or other plant-based milk (UK)
- Toppings of choice: granola, sliced fruits, nuts, seeds, coconut flakes, etc.

Instructions:

1. In a blender, combine the mixed berries, frozen banana, and almond milk.
2. Blend until smooth and creamy, adding more almond milk if needed to reach your desired consistency.
3. Pour the smoothie into a bowl.
4. Top with your favorite toppings, such as granola, sliced fruits, nuts, seeds, or coconut flakes.
5. Serve immediately and enjoy this refreshing and nutritious smoothie bowl for breakfast or as a snack!

Nutritional Info (per serving, excluding toppings): Calories: 180 Fat: 2g Carbs: 40g Protein: 3g

Coconut Cinnamon Quinoa Porridge

Prep: 5 mins | Cook: 20 mins | Serves: 2

Ingredients:

- 1/2 cup quinoa (US) / 90g quinoa (UK)
- 1 cup coconut milk (US) / 240ml coconut milk (UK)
- 1/2 cup water (US) / 120ml water (UK)
- 1/2 tsp ground cinnamon
- 1/4 cup shredded coconut (US) / 20g shredded coconut (UK)
- Maple syrup or honey, to taste

Instructions:

1. Rinse the quinoa under cold water in a fine-mesh strainer.
2. In a saucepan, combine the rinsed quinoa, coconut milk, water, and ground cinnamon.

3. Bring the mixture to a boil, then reduce the heat to low. Simmer, covered, for about 15-20 minutes, or until the quinoa is cooked and the mixture thickens, stirring occasionally.
4. Once the porridge reaches your desired consistency, remove from heat.
5. Stir in the shredded coconut and sweeten with maple syrup or honey to taste.
6. Divide the porridge into serving bowls and garnish with additional shredded coconut or a sprinkle of cinnamon if desired.
7. Serve warm and enjoy this creamy and flavorful quinoa porridge for a satisfying breakfast or snack!

Nutritional Info (per serving): Calories: 280 Fat: 18g Carbs: 25g Protein: 6g

Spinach Bell Pepper Frittata Bites

Prep: 10 mins | Cook: 20 mins | Serves: 4 (makes 12 bites)

Ingredients:

- 6 large eggs
- 1/4 cup almond milk or other plant-based milk (US) / 60ml almond milk or other plant-based milk (UK)
- 1 cup fresh spinach, chopped (US) / 80g fresh spinach, chopped (UK)
- 1/2 bell pepper, diced (any color)
- Salt and pepper to taste
- Cooking spray or olive oil for greasing

Instructions:

1. Preheat the oven to 350°F (180°C). Grease a mini muffin tin with cooking spray or olive oil.
2. In a mixing bowl, whisk together the eggs and almond milk until well combined.
3. Stir in the chopped spinach and diced bell pepper. Season with salt and pepper to taste.
4. Pour the egg mixture evenly into the prepared mini muffin tin, filling each cup about 3/4 full.
5. Bake in the preheated oven for 15-20 minutes, or until the frittata bites are set and lightly golden brown on top.
6. Remove from the oven and allow to cool slightly before carefully removing the frittata bites from the muffin tin.
7. Serve warm or at room temperature as a delicious and nutritious breakfast or snack option!

Nutritional Info (per serving, 3 frittata bites): Calories: 120 Fat: 8g Carbs: 2g Protein: 10g

Mushroom Onion Tofu Scramble

Prep: 10 mins | Cook: 10 mins | Serves: 2

Ingredients:

- 1 block (14 oz) firm tofu, drained and pressed (US) / 400g block firm tofu, drained and pressed (UK)
- 1 cup sliced mushrooms (US) / 150g sliced mushrooms (UK)
- 1 small onion, diced
- 2 cloves garlic, minced
- 2 tbsp nutritional yeast
- 1/2 tsp turmeric powder
- Salt and pepper to taste
- Fresh parsley or chives for garnish (optional)
- Cooking spray or olive oil for cooking

Instructions:

1. Heat a non-stick skillet over medium heat and lightly grease with cooking spray or olive oil.
2. Crumble the pressed tofu into the skillet using your hands or a fork, breaking it up into small pieces resembling scrambled eggs.
3. Cook the tofu for 3-5 minutes, stirring occasionally, until it starts to brown slightly.
4. Add the sliced mushrooms, diced onion, and minced garlic to the skillet. Cook for another 5 minutes, or until the vegetables are softened and the tofu is lightly golden.
5. Sprinkle the nutritional yeast and turmeric powder over the tofu and vegetables. Season with salt and pepper to taste.
6. Stir everything together and cook for another 2-3 minutes, allowing the flavors to meld.
7. Remove from heat and garnish with fresh parsley or chives if desired.
8. Serve hot as a hearty and protein-packed breakfast option or enjoy as a filling meal any time of day!

Nutritional Info (per serving): Calories: 200 Fat: 10g Carbs: 10g Protein: 20g

Berrylicious Chia Pudding Parfait

Prep: 5 mins | Cook: 4 hours (chilling time) | Serves: 2

Ingredients:

- 1/4 cup chia seeds (US) / 40g chia seeds (UK)
- 1 cup almond milk or other plant-based milk (US) / 240ml almond milk or other plant-based milk (UK)

- 1/2 tsp vanilla extract
- 1 tbsp maple syrup or honey (optional)
- 1/2 cup mixed berries (US) / 75g mixed berries (UK)
- 2 tbsp granola for topping (optional)

Instructions:

1. In a mixing bowl or jar, combine the chia seeds, almond milk, vanilla extract, and maple syrup or honey if using. Stir well to combine.
2. Cover the bowl or jar and refrigerate for at least 4 hours or overnight, allowing the chia seeds to absorb the liquid and thicken into a pudding-like consistency.
3. Once the chia pudding has set, give it a good stir to break up any clumps and ensure a smooth texture.
4. To assemble the parfait, layer the chia pudding with mixed berries in serving glasses or bowls.
5. Repeat the layers until all the pudding and berries are used up, ending with a layer of berries on top.
6. Optionally, sprinkle granola over the top for added crunch and texture.
7. Serve chilled and enjoy this delightful and nutritious chia pudding parfait for breakfast, dessert, or a satisfying snack!

Nutritional Info (per serving): Calories: 180 Fat: 7g Carbs: 25g Protein: 5g

Nutty Banana Toast

Prep: 5 mins | Cook: 5 mins | Serves: 2

Ingredients:

- 2 slices whole grain bread (US) / 2 slices wholemeal bread (UK)
- 2 tbsp nut butter (such as almond or peanut butter)
- 1 ripe banana, sliced
- 1 tbsp chia seeds (optional)
- Drizzle of honey or maple syrup (optional)

Instructions:

1. Toast the slices of bread until golden brown and crispy.
2. Spread each slice with a tablespoon of nut butter.
3. Arrange the sliced banana evenly over the nut butter.
4. Sprinkle chia seeds over the banana slices, if using.
5. Drizzle with honey or maple syrup for added sweetness, if desired.
6. Serve immediately for a simple yet satisfying breakfast or snack option!

Nutritional Info (per serving): Calories: 250 Fat: 10g Carbs: 35g Protein: 7g

Yogurt Fruit Salad Bowl

Prep: 10 mins | Serves: 2

Ingredients:

- 1 cup plain yogurt (US) / 240g plain yogurt (UK)
- 1 cup mixed fresh fruits (such as berries, kiwi, mango, and pineapple), diced (US) / 150g mixed fresh fruits, diced (UK)
- 2 tbsp granola or chopped nuts for topping (optional)
- Drizzle of honey or maple syrup (optional)

Instructions:

1. Divide the plain yogurt evenly between two serving bowls.
2. Arrange the diced mixed fruits on top of the yogurt.
3. Sprinkle granola or chopped nuts over the fruit, if using, for added texture and crunch.
4. Drizzle with honey or maple syrup for extra sweetness, if desired.
5. Serve immediately for a refreshing and nutritious breakfast or snack option!

Nutritional Info (per serving): Calories: 180 Fat: 5g Carbs: 30g Protein: 8g

Savory Sweet Potato Hash

Prep: 10 mins | Cook: 25 mins | Serves: 2

Ingredients:

- 2 medium sweet potatoes, peeled and diced (US) / 400g sweet potatoes, peeled and diced (UK)
- 1 small onion, diced
- 1 bell pepper, diced
- 2 cloves garlic, minced
- 2 tbsp olive oil
- Salt and pepper to taste
- 4 eggs
- Fresh parsley or chives for garnish (optional)

Instructions:

1. Heat olive oil in a large skillet over medium heat.
2. Add diced sweet potatoes to the skillet and cook for about 10-12 minutes, stirring occasionally, until they start to soften.

3. Add diced onion, bell pepper, and minced garlic to the skillet. Cook for another 8-10 minutes, or until vegetables are tender and sweet potatoes are cooked through.
4. Season with salt and pepper to taste.
5. Create four wells in the sweet potato mixture and crack one egg into each well.
6. Cover the skillet and cook for 5-7 minutes, or until eggs are cooked to your desired doneness.
7. Garnish with fresh parsley or chives if desired.
8. Serve hot and enjoy this hearty and flavorful sweet potato hash for breakfast or brunch!

Nutritional Info (per serving): Calories: 350 Fat: 16g Carbs: 40g Protein: 14g

Apple Cinnamon Overnight Oats

Prep: 5 mins | Chill: 4 hours | Serves: 2

Ingredients:

- 1 cup rolled oats (US) / 100g rolled oats (UK)
- 1 cup almond milk or other plant-based milk (US) / 240ml almond milk or other plant-based milk (UK)
- 1/2 cup unsweetened applesauce
- 1/4 cup raisins
- 1/2 tsp ground cinnamon
- 1 tbsp maple syrup or honey (optional)

Instructions:

1. In a mixing bowl or jar, combine rolled oats, almond milk, unsweetened applesauce, raisins, and ground cinnamon.
2. Stir well to combine all ingredients.
3. Cover the bowl or jar and refrigerate for at least 4 hours or overnight.
4. Once chilled, give the oats a good stir to mix everything together.
5. Optionally, drizzle with maple syrup or honey for extra sweetness.
6. Serve cold and enjoy this convenient and nutritious breakfast option!

Nutritional Info (per serving): Calories: 250 Fat: 3g Carbs: 47g Protein: 9g

Nutty Zucchini Bread

Prep: 15 mins | Cook: 50 mins | Serves: 8

Ingredients:

- 1 1/2 cups grated zucchini (US) / 200g grated zucchini (UK)
- 1 1/2 cups whole wheat flour (US) / 180g wholemeal flour (UK)
- 1/2 cup coconut sugar or brown sugar
- 1/4 cup unsweetened applesauce
- 1/4 cup olive oil or melted coconut oil
- 2 eggs
- 1 tsp baking powder
- 1/2 tsp baking soda
- 1 tsp ground cinnamon
- 1/2 tsp ground nutmeg
- 1/4 tsp salt
- 1/2 cup chopped walnuts (US) / 40g chopped walnuts (UK)
- 1/2 cup raisins (US) / 75g raisins (UK)

Instructions:

1. Preheat the oven to 350°F (180°C). Grease a 9x5-inch loaf pan with cooking spray or line with parchment paper.
2. In a large mixing bowl, combine grated zucchini, whole wheat flour, coconut sugar, applesauce, olive oil or melted coconut oil, eggs, baking powder, baking soda, cinnamon, nutmeg, and salt. Stir until well combined.
3. Fold in chopped walnuts and raisins until evenly distributed in the batter.
4. Pour the batter into the prepared loaf pan and spread it out evenly.
5. Bake in the preheated oven for 45-50 minutes, or until a toothpick inserted into the center comes out clean.
6. Remove from the oven and allow the zucchini bread to cool in the pan for 10 minutes before transferring it to a wire rack to cool completely.
7. Once cooled, slice and serve this delicious and moist zucchini bread as a nutritious breakfast or snack option!

Nutritional Info (per serving): Calories: 220 Fat: 8g Carbs: 35g Protein: 5g

Vegan Pancakes with Maple Syrup

Prep: 10 mins | Cook: 10 mins | Serves: 2 (makes about 6 pancakes)

Ingredients:

- 1 cup whole wheat flour (US) / 120g wholemeal flour (UK)
- 1 ripe banana, mashed
- 1 cup almond milk or other plant-based milk (US) / 240ml almond milk or other plant-based milk (UK)
- 1 tbsp maple syrup
- 1 tsp baking powder
- 1/2 tsp ground cinnamon
- Cooking spray or olive oil for cooking

Instructions:

1. In a mixing bowl, combine the whole wheat flour, mashed banana, almond milk, maple syrup, baking powder, and ground cinnamon. Stir until just combined.
2. Heat a non-stick skillet or griddle over medium heat and lightly grease with cooking spray or olive oil.
3. Pour about 1/4 cup of batter onto the skillet for each pancake. Cook for 2-3 minutes, or until bubbles form on the surface and the edges begin to set.
4. Flip the pancakes and cook for an additional 2-3 minutes on the other side, or until golden brown and cooked through.
5. Repeat with the remaining batter, adding more cooking spray or olive oil to the skillet as needed.
6. Serve the pancakes warm with maple syrup and fresh fruit for a delicious and nutritious breakfast treat!

Nutritional Info (per serving, 3 pancakes): Calories: 300 Fat: 8g Carbs: 45g Protein: 8g

Plant-Powered Breakfast Burrito

Prep: 15 mins | Cook: 10 mins | Serves: 2

Ingredients:

- 2 whole grain tortillas (US) / 2 wholemeal tortillas (UK)
- 1 cup firm tofu, crumbled
- 1/2 cup black beans, drained and rinsed (US) / 100g black beans, drained and rinsed (UK)
- 1/2 cup bell peppers, diced
- 1/4 cup red onion, diced

- 1/2 tsp ground cumin
- 1/2 tsp chili powder
- Salt and pepper to taste
- Cooking spray or olive oil for cooking

Instructions:

1. Heat a non-stick skillet over medium heat and lightly grease with cooking spray or olive oil.
2. Add diced bell peppers and red onion to the skillet. Cook for 3-4 minutes, or until vegetables start to soften.
3. Add crumbled tofu, black beans, ground cumin, chili powder, salt, and pepper to the skillet. Cook for another 5-6 minutes, stirring occasionally, until tofu is heated through and lightly browned.
4. Warm the tortillas in the skillet for about 30 seconds on each side.
5. Divide the tofu and black bean mixture evenly between the warmed tortillas.
6. Roll up the tortillas, folding in the sides to enclose the filling.
7. Serve immediately for a protein-packed and satisfying breakfast option!

Nutritional Info (per serving): Calories: 350 Fat: 10g Carbs: 45g Protein: 18g

Acai Bowl with Granola

Prep: 5 mins | Serves: 1

Ingredients:

- 1 frozen banana, sliced
- 1 pack frozen acai puree (unsweetened)
- 1/2 cup mixed berries (US) / 75g mixed berries (UK)
- 1/2 cup almond milk or other plant-based milk (US) / 120ml almond milk or other plant-based milk (UK)
- Toppings: granola, sliced fruits, nuts, seeds, coconut flakes, etc.

Instructions:

1. In a blender, combine frozen banana, frozen acai puree, mixed berries, and almond milk.
2. Blend until smooth and creamy, adding more almond milk if needed to reach desired consistency.
3. Pour the acai mixture into a bowl.
4. Top with your favorite toppings, such as granola, sliced fruits, nuts, seeds, or coconut flakes.

5. Serve immediately and enjoy this refreshing and nutrient-packed acai bowl for breakfast or as a snack!

Nutritional Info (per serving, excluding toppings): Calories: 200 Fat: 5g Carbs: 40g Protein: 3g

SALADS AND APPETIZERS

Beet, Orange, and Walnut Salad

Prep: 15 mins | Serves: 2

Ingredients:

- 4 cups mixed greens (US) / 120g mixed greens (UK)
- 1 large beet, roasted and sliced
- 1 orange, peeled and segmented
- 1/4 cup walnuts, chopped (US) / 30g walnuts, chopped (UK)
- Balsamic vinaigrette dressing

Instructions:

1. Arrange mixed greens on a serving platter or in individual bowls.
2. Top with roasted beet slices and orange segments.
3. Sprinkle chopped walnuts over the salad.
4. Drizzle with balsamic vinaigrette dressing.
5. Serve immediately as a refreshing and nutritious appetizer or side salad.

Nutritional Info (per serving): Calories: 180 Fat: 8g Carbs: 25g Protein: 5g

Quinoa Salad with Roasted Vegetables and Avocado

Prep: 20 mins | Cook: 25 mins | Serves: 4

Ingredients:

- 1 cup quinoa (US) / 180g quinoa (UK)
- 2 cups mixed vegetables (such as bell peppers, zucchini, and cherry tomatoes), chopped
- 1 avocado, diced
- 2 tbsp olive oil
- Salt and pepper to taste
- Lemon tahini dressing

Instructions:

1. Preheat the oven to 400°F (200°C).
2. Cook quinoa according to package instructions and let cool.
3. Toss chopped vegetables with olive oil, salt, and pepper on a baking sheet.
4. Roast vegetables in the preheated oven for 20-25 minutes, or until tender and slightly caramelized.

5. In a large mixing bowl, combine cooked quinoa, roasted vegetables, and diced avocado.
6. Drizzle with lemon tahini dressing and toss to coat evenly.
7. Serve chilled or at room temperature as a hearty and nutritious salad.

Nutritional Info (per serving): Calories: 300 Fat: 15g Carbs: 35g Protein: 8g

Caprese Salad with Tomato, Mozzarella, and Basil

Prep: 10 mins | Serves: 2

Ingredients:

- 2 large tomatoes, sliced
- 1 ball fresh mozzarella, sliced
- Handful of fresh basil leaves
- Balsamic glaze
- Extra virgin olive oil
- Salt and pepper to taste

Instructions:

1. Arrange tomato and mozzarella slices on a serving platter or individual plates, alternating them.
2. Tuck fresh basil leaves between tomato and mozzarella slices.
3. Drizzle with balsamic glaze and extra virgin olive oil.
4. Season with salt and pepper to taste.
5. Serve immediately as a classic and elegant appetizer or side salad.

Nutritional Info (per serving): Calories: 250 Fat: 18g Carbs: 5g Protein: 15g

Cucumber and Tomato Salad with Lemon Dressing

Prep: 10 mins | Serves: 2

Ingredients:

- 1 cucumber, sliced
- 2 tomatoes, diced
- 1/4 red onion, thinly sliced
- Handful of fresh parsley, chopped
- Juice of 1 lemon
- 2 tbsp extra virgin olive oil
- Salt and pepper to taste

Instructions:

1. In a large mixing bowl, combine cucumber slices, diced tomatoes, sliced red onion, and chopped parsley.
2. In a small bowl, whisk together lemon juice and extra virgin olive oil to make the dressing.
3. Drizzle the dressing over the salad and toss to coat evenly.
4. Season with salt and pepper to taste.
5. Serve immediately as a light and refreshing salad.

Nutritional Info (per serving): Calories: 150 Fat: 10g Carbs: 15g Protein: 3g

Black Bean and Corn Salad with Cilantro Lime Dressing

Prep: 15 mins | Serves: 4

Ingredients:

- 1 can black beans, drained and rinsed (US) / 400g black beans, drained and rinsed (UK)
- 1 cup corn kernels, fresh or frozen (US) / 150g corn kernels, fresh or frozen (UK)
- 1 red bell pepper, diced
- 1/4 cup red onion, finely chopped
- 1/4 cup fresh cilantro, chopped
- Juice of 2 limes
- 2 tbsp olive oil
- 1 tsp honey or maple syrup
- Salt and pepper to taste
- Optional: diced avocado for garnish

Instructions:

1. In a large mixing bowl, combine black beans, corn kernels, diced red bell pepper, chopped red onion, and chopped cilantro.
2. In a small bowl, whisk together lime juice, olive oil, honey or maple syrup, salt, and pepper to make the dressing.
3. Pour the dressing over the salad and toss to coat evenly.
4. Garnish with diced avocado if desired.
5. Serve chilled or at room temperature as a flavorful and protein-packed salad.

Nutritional Info (per serving): Calories: 200 Fat: 8g Carbs: 28g Protein: 6g

Hummus with Raw Vegetables and Pita Bread

Prep: 10 mins | Serves: 4

Ingredients:

- 1 cup hummus (store-bought or homemade)
- Assorted raw vegetables (such as carrots, cucumbers, bell peppers, cherry tomatoes)
- Pita bread, sliced into wedges
- Optional: olives for garnish

Instructions:

1. Arrange hummus in a serving bowl or platter.
2. Wash and prepare raw vegetables by cutting them into sticks or bite-sized pieces.
3. Place the raw vegetables around the hummus bowl.
4. Arrange pita bread wedges on the side.
5. Optionally, garnish with olives for extra flavor.
6. Serve immediately as a healthy and satisfying snack or appetizer.

Nutritional Info (per serving): Calories: 180 Fat: 6g Carbs: 28g Protein: 6g

Guacamole with Baked Tortilla Chips

Prep: 15 mins | Cook: 10 mins | Serves: 4

Ingredients:

- 2 ripe avocados
- 1 tomato, diced
- 1/4 red onion, finely chopped
- 1 jalapeño pepper, seeded and minced
- Juice of 1 lime
- Handful of fresh cilantro, chopped
- Salt and pepper to taste
- 4 whole grain tortillas (US) / 4 wholemeal tortillas (UK)

Instructions:

1. Preheat the oven to 375°F (190°C).
2. In a mixing bowl, mash ripe avocados with a fork until smooth.
3. Stir in diced tomato, chopped red onion, minced jalapeño pepper, lime juice, and chopped cilantro.
4. Season with salt and pepper to taste.

5. Cut whole grain tortillas into wedges and arrange them in a single layer on a baking sheet.
6. Bake tortilla chips in the preheated oven for 8-10 minutes, or until crispy and golden brown.
7. Serve guacamole with baked tortilla chips as a delicious and wholesome snack or appetizer.

Nutritional Info (per serving): Calories: 220 Fat: 12g Carbs: 27g Protein: 5g

Roasted Vegetable Skewers with Balsamic Glaze

Prep: 15 mins | Cook: 20 mins | Serves: 4

Ingredients:

- 2 bell peppers (any color), cut into chunks
- 1 zucchini, sliced into rounds
- 1 yellow squash, sliced into rounds
- 1 red onion, cut into chunks
- 8 cherry tomatoes
- 8 wooden skewers, soaked in water for 30 minutes
- 2 tbsp olive oil
- Salt and pepper to taste
- Balsamic glaze for drizzling

Instructions:

1. Preheat the oven to 400°F (200°C).
2. Thread the bell pepper chunks, zucchini slices, yellow squash slices, red onion chunks, and cherry tomatoes onto the soaked wooden skewers, alternating the vegetables.
3. Place the skewers on a baking sheet lined with parchment paper.
4. Drizzle the skewers with olive oil and season with salt and pepper.
5. Roast in the preheated oven for 15-20 minutes, or until the vegetables are tender and slightly charred, turning halfway through cooking.
6. Remove from the oven and transfer the skewers to a serving platter.
7. Drizzle with balsamic glaze before serving.
8. Serve immediately as a flavorful and colorful appetizer or side dish.

Nutritional Info (per serving): Calories: 120 Fat: 6g Carbs: 16g Protein: 2g

Watermelon and Feta Salad with Mint

Prep: 10 mins | Serves: 4

Ingredients:

- 4 cups cubed watermelon (US) / 400g cubed watermelon (UK)
- 1/2 cup crumbled feta cheese (US) / 100g crumbled feta cheese (UK)
- Handful of fresh mint leaves, torn
- Juice of 1 lime
- Drizzle of honey (optional)

Instructions:

1. In a large mixing bowl, combine cubed watermelon, crumbled feta cheese, and torn mint leaves.
2. Squeeze lime juice over the salad and toss gently to combine.
3. Optionally, drizzle with honey for a touch of sweetness.
4. Serve immediately as a refreshing and vibrant salad.

Nutritional Info (per serving): Calories: 100 Fat: 4g Carbs: 15g Protein: 3g

Lentil and Roasted Vegetable Salad

Prep: 15 mins | Cook: 25 mins | Serves: 4

Ingredients:

- 1 cup green lentils (US) / 200g green lentils (UK)
- 2 cups mixed vegetables (such as carrots, bell peppers, and cherry tomatoes), chopped
- 2 tbsp olive oil
- Salt and pepper to taste
- Lemon tahini dressing
- Optional: crumbled feta cheese for garnish

Instructions:

1. Cook green lentils according to package instructions and let cool.
2. Preheat the oven to 400°F (200°C).
3. Toss chopped vegetables with olive oil, salt, and pepper on a baking sheet.
4. Roast vegetables in the preheated oven for 20-25 minutes, or until tender and slightly caramelized.
5. In a large mixing bowl, combine cooked lentils and roasted vegetables.
6. Drizzle with lemon tahini dressing and toss to coat evenly.
7. Optionally, garnish with crumbled feta cheese before serving.

8. Serve chilled or at room temperature as a hearty and nutritious salad.

Nutritional Info (per serving): Calories: 250 Fat: 10g Carbs: 30g Protein: 10g

Spinach and Strawberry Salad with Poppy Seed Dressing

Prep: 10 mins | Serves: 4

Ingredients:

- 6 cups fresh spinach leaves (US) / 180g fresh spinach leaves (UK)
- 1 cup sliced strawberries
- 1/4 cup sliced almonds (US) / 30g sliced almonds (UK)
- 1/4 cup crumbled feta cheese (US) / 50g crumbled feta cheese (UK)
- Poppy seed dressing

Instructions:

1. In a large mixing bowl, combine fresh spinach leaves, sliced strawberries, sliced almonds, and crumbled feta cheese.
2. Drizzle with poppy seed dressing.
3. Toss gently to coat the salad ingredients evenly with the dressing.
4. Serve immediately as a delightful and nutritious salad.

Nutritional Info (per serving): Calories: 150 Fat: 10g Carbs: 10g Protein: 6g

Mediterranean Chickpea Salad with Olives and Feta

Prep: 15 mins | Serves: 4

Ingredients:

- 1 can chickpeas, drained and rinsed (US) / 400g chickpeas, drained and rinsed (UK)
- 1 cup cherry tomatoes, halved
- 1/4 cup sliced Kalamata olives
- 1/4 cup crumbled feta cheese (US) / 50g crumbled feta cheese (UK)
- Handful of fresh parsley, chopped
- Juice of 1 lemon
- 2 tbsp extra virgin olive oil
- Salt and pepper to taste

Instructions:

1. In a large mixing bowl, combine chickpeas, cherry tomatoes, sliced Kalamata olives, crumbled feta cheese, and chopped fresh parsley.
2. Drizzle with lemon juice and extra virgin olive oil.
3. Season with salt and pepper to taste.

4. Toss gently to combine all the ingredients.
5. Serve chilled or at room temperature as a flavorful and satisfying salad.

Nutritional Info (per serving): Calories: 220 Fat: 12g Carbs: 20g Protein: 8g

Avocado and Grapefruit Salad with Lime Vinaigrette

Prep: 10 mins | Serves: 2

Ingredients:

- 2 cups mixed salad greens (US) / 60g mixed salad greens (UK)
- 1 avocado, sliced
- 1 grapefruit, segmented
- 2 tbsp chopped pistachios (US) / 20g chopped pistachios (UK)
- Lime vinaigrette

Instructions:

1. Arrange mixed salad greens on serving plates.
2. Top with sliced avocado and grapefruit segments.
3. Sprinkle chopped pistachios over the salad.
4. Drizzle with lime vinaigrette.
5. Serve immediately as a refreshing and vibrant salad.

Nutritional Info (per serving): Calories: 250 Fat: 18g Carbs: 20g Protein: 5g

Grilled Peach and Arugula Salad with Balsamic Reduction

Prep: 10 mins | Cook: 5 mins | Serves: 2

Ingredients:

- 2 ripe peaches, halved and pitted
- 2 cups arugula (US) / 60g arugula (UK)
- 1/4 cup crumbled goat cheese (US) / 50g crumbled goat cheese (UK)
- Balsamic reduction

Instructions:

1. Preheat a grill or grill pan over medium-high heat.
2. Place peach halves on the grill, cut side down, and cook for 3-4 minutes, or until grill marks appear and peaches are slightly softened.
3. Arrange arugula on serving plates.
4. Top with grilled peach halves and crumbled goat cheese.
5. Drizzle with balsamic reduction.
6. Serve immediately as a delicious and elegant salad.

Nutritional Info (per serving): Calories: 200 Fat: 8g Carbs: 30g Protein: 6g

Vegetable Spring Rolls with Peanut Dipping Sauce

Prep: 30 mins | Cook: 10 mins | Serves: 4

Ingredients:

- For the Spring Rolls:
- 8 rice paper wrappers
- 2 cups mixed vegetables (such as shredded carrots, cucumber, bell peppers, lettuce, and avocado)
- Handful of fresh herbs (such as mint, basil, and cilantro)
- Rice noodles, cooked according to package instructions
  For the Peanut Dipping Sauce:
- 1/4 cup peanut butter
- 2 tbsp soy sauce
- 1 tbsp rice vinegar
- 1 tbsp maple syrup or honey
- 1 garlic clove, minced
- 1/2 tsp grated ginger
- Water, as needed to thin the sauce

Instructions:

1. Prepare all the vegetables and herbs for the spring rolls by washing, peeling, and slicing them into thin strips.
2. Fill a shallow dish with warm water. Dip one rice paper wrapper into the water for about 5-10 seconds until it softens.
3. Place the softened rice paper wrapper on a clean surface.
4. Arrange a small amount of cooked rice noodles, mixed vegetables, and fresh herbs in the center of the wrapper.
5. Fold the bottom of the wrapper over the filling, then fold the sides in, and roll tightly to enclose the filling.
6. Repeat with the remaining wrappers and filling ingredients.
7. To make the peanut dipping sauce, whisk together peanut butter, soy sauce, rice vinegar, maple syrup or honey, minced garlic, and grated ginger in a small bowl. Add water gradually until desired consistency is reached.
8. Serve the vegetable spring rolls with the peanut dipping sauce on the side.
9. Enjoy these refreshing and crunchy spring rolls as a healthy appetizer or snack.

Nutritional Info (per serving, including dipping sauce): Calories: 250 Fat: 12g Carbs: 30g Protein: 8g

SOUPS AND STEWS

Vegetable Minestrone Soup

Prep: 15 mins | Cook: 30 mins | Serves: 6

Ingredients:

- 2 tbsp olive oil
- 1 onion, diced
- 2 carrots, diced
- 2 celery stalks, diced
- 2 garlic cloves, minced
- 1 can (14 oz) diced tomatoes (US) / 400g canned diced tomatoes (UK)
- 6 cups vegetable broth
- 1 cup pasta shells
- 1 can (15 oz) kidney beans, drained and rinsed (US) / 400g canned kidney beans, drained and rinsed (UK)
- 2 cups chopped spinach
- Salt and pepper to taste
- Grated Parmesan cheese for serving (optional)

Instructions:

1. In a large pot, heat olive oil over medium heat.
2. Add diced onion, carrots, celery, and minced garlic. Cook until softened, about 5-7 minutes.
3. Stir in diced tomatoes and vegetable broth. Bring to a simmer.
4. Add pasta shells and kidney beans. Cook for 10 minutes, or until pasta is al dente.
5. Stir in chopped spinach and cook until wilted, about 2 minutes.
6. Season with salt and pepper to taste.
7. Serve hot, garnished with grated Parmesan cheese if desired.
8. Enjoy this hearty and nutritious minestrone soup!

Nutritional Info (per serving): Calories: 200 Fat: 5g Carbs: 30g Protein: 8g

Lentil and Sweet Potato Stew

Prep: 15 mins | Cook: 40 mins | Serves: 4

Ingredients:

- 1 tbsp olive oil
- 1 onion, diced

- 2 garlic cloves, minced
- 2 carrots, diced
- 2 sweet potatoes, peeled and diced
- 1 cup dried green lentils, rinsed
- 4 cups vegetable broth
- 1 tsp ground cumin
- 1/2 tsp smoked paprika
- Salt and pepper to taste
- Fresh parsley for garnish (optional)

Instructions:

1. In a large pot, heat olive oil over medium heat.
2. Add diced onion and minced garlic. Cook until fragrant, about 2 minutes.
3. Stir in diced carrots and sweet potatoes. Cook for 5 minutes.
4. Add dried green lentils, vegetable broth, ground cumin, and smoked paprika. Bring to a boil.
5. Reduce heat to low, cover, and simmer for 30 minutes, or until lentils and vegetables are tender.
6. Season with salt and pepper to taste.
7. Serve hot, garnished with fresh parsley if desired.
8. Enjoy this comforting and filling lentil and sweet potato stew!

Nutritional Info (per serving): Calories: 250 Fat: 3g Carbs: 45g Protein: 10g

Tomato Basil Soup with Grilled Cheese Croutons

Prep: 10 mins | Cook: 30 mins | Serves: 4

Ingredients:

- 2 tbsp olive oil
- 1 onion, diced
- 2 garlic cloves, minced
- 2 cans (14 oz each) diced tomatoes (US) / 800g canned diced tomatoes (UK)
- 2 cups vegetable broth
- 1/4 cup chopped fresh basil
- Salt and pepper to taste
- 4 slices bread
- 4 slices cheese (cheddar or mozzarella)
- Butter for spreading

Instructions:

1. In a large pot, heat olive oil over medium heat.
2. Add diced onion and minced garlic. Cook until softened, about 5 minutes.
3. Stir in diced tomatoes and vegetable broth. Bring to a simmer.
4. Add chopped fresh basil. Cook for 15 minutes.
5. Using an immersion blender, blend the soup until smooth. Alternatively, transfer the soup to a blender and blend until smooth, then return to the pot.
6. Season with salt and pepper to taste.
7. Heat a skillet over medium heat. Spread butter on one side of each bread slice.
8. Place bread slices, buttered side down, in the skillet. Top each slice with a slice of cheese.
9. Cook until bread is golden brown and cheese is melted.
10. Remove from heat and slice each grilled cheese sandwich into bite-sized croutons.
11. Serve the tomato basil soup hot, topped with grilled cheese croutons.
12. Enjoy this classic combination of flavors!

Nutritional Info (per serving): Calories: 300 Fat: 12g Carbs: 35g Protein: 10g

Vegan Chili with Avocado and Cilantro

Prep: 15 mins | Cook: 40 mins | Serves: 6

Ingredients:

- 1 tbsp olive oil
- 1 onion, diced
- 2 cloves garlic, minced
- 1 bell pepper, diced
- 1 zucchini, diced
- 1 cup corn kernels (fresh or frozen)
- 2 cans (14 oz each) black beans, drained and rinsed (US) / 400g canned black beans, drained and rinsed (UK)
- 2 cans (14 oz each) diced tomatoes (US) / 400g canned diced tomatoes (UK)
- 2 cups vegetable broth
- 2 tbsp chili powder
- 1 tsp ground cumin
- Salt and pepper to taste
- 1 avocado, diced, for serving
- Fresh cilantro, chopped, for serving
- Lime wedges, for serving

Instructions:

1. Heat olive oil in a large pot over medium heat.
2. Add diced onion and minced garlic. Cook until softened, about 5 minutes.
3. Stir in diced bell pepper and zucchini. Cook for another 5 minutes.
4. Add corn kernels, black beans, diced tomatoes, vegetable broth, chili powder, and ground cumin. Stir to combine.
5. Bring the chili to a simmer, then reduce heat to low and cover. Let it simmer for 30 minutes, stirring occasionally.
6. Season with salt and pepper to taste.
7. Serve the vegan chili hot, topped with diced avocado and chopped cilantro.
8. Squeeze fresh lime juice over each serving before enjoying.
9. This flavorful vegan chili is perfect for a cozy meal!

Nutritional Info (per serving): Calories: 250 Fat: 8g Carbs: 40g Protein: 10g

Butternut Squash and Apple Soup

Prep: 15 mins | Cook: 30 mins | Serves: 4

Ingredients:

- 1 tbsp olive oil
- 1 onion, diced
- 2 cloves garlic, minced
- 1 butternut squash, peeled, seeded, and diced
- 2 apples, peeled, cored, and diced
- 4 cups vegetable broth
- 1/2 tsp ground cinnamon
- 1/4 tsp ground nutmeg
- Salt and pepper to taste
- Coconut milk for drizzling (optional)
- Toasted pumpkin seeds for garnish (optional)

Instructions:

1. Heat olive oil in a large pot over medium heat.
2. Add diced onion and minced garlic. Cook until softened, about 5 minutes.
3. Add diced butternut squash and apples to the pot. Cook for another 5 minutes.
4. Pour in vegetable broth, ground cinnamon, and ground nutmeg. Stir to combine.
5. Bring the soup to a boil, then reduce heat to low and cover. Let it simmer for 20 minutes, or until the squash and apples are tender.

6. Using an immersion blender, blend the soup until smooth. Alternatively, transfer the soup to a blender and blend until smooth, then return to the pot.
7. Season with salt and pepper to taste.
8. Serve the butternut squash and apple soup hot, drizzled with coconut milk and garnished with toasted pumpkin seeds if desired.
9. Enjoy the cozy flavors of fall in every spoonful!

Nutritional Info (per serving): Calories: 200 Fat: 5g Carbs: 40g Protein: 3g

White Bean and Kale Soup

Prep: 15 mins | Cook: 35 mins | Serves: 6

Ingredients:

- 2 tbsp olive oil
- 1 onion, diced
- 2 cloves garlic, minced
- 2 carrots, diced
- 2 celery stalks, diced
- 1 can (14 oz) white beans, drained and rinsed (US) / 400g canned white beans, drained and rinsed (UK)
- 1 bunch kale, stems removed and leaves chopped
- 6 cups vegetable broth
- 1 tsp dried thyme
- 1 bay leaf
- Salt and pepper to taste
- Lemon wedges for serving

Instructions:

1. Heat olive oil in a large pot over medium heat.
2. Add diced onion and minced garlic. Cook until softened, about 5 minutes.
3. Stir in diced carrots and celery. Cook for another 5 minutes.
4. Add white beans, chopped kale, vegetable broth, dried thyme, and bay leaf to the pot. Stir to combine.
5. Bring the soup to a simmer, then reduce heat to low and cover. Let it simmer for 25 minutes, stirring occasionally.
6. Season with salt and pepper to taste.
7. Remove the bay leaf before serving.
8. Serve the white bean and kale soup hot, with lemon wedges on the side for squeezing.
9. Enjoy this hearty and nutritious soup as a comforting meal!

Nutritional Info (per serving): Calories: 180 Fat: 5g Carbs: 25g Protein: 8g

Cauliflower and Potato Soup with Crispy Chickpeas

Prep: 15 mins | Cook: 40 mins | Serves: 6

Ingredients:

- 2 tbsp olive oil
- 1 onion, diced
- 2 cloves garlic, minced
- 1 head cauliflower, chopped into florets
- 2 potatoes, peeled and diced
- 4 cups vegetable broth
- 1 can (14 oz) chickpeas, drained and rinsed (US) / 400g canned chickpeas, drained and rinsed (UK)
- 1 tsp smoked paprika
- Salt and pepper to taste
- Fresh parsley for garnish (optional)

Instructions:

1. Heat olive oil in a large pot over medium heat.
2. Add diced onion and minced garlic. Cook until softened, about 5 minutes.
3. Add cauliflower florets and diced potatoes to the pot. Cook for another 5 minutes.
4. Pour in vegetable broth. Bring to a boil, then reduce heat to low and cover. Let it simmer for 25 minutes, or until vegetables are tender.
5. While the soup is simmering, preheat the oven to 400°F (200°C).
6. Spread drained and rinsed chickpeas on a baking sheet lined with parchment paper. Sprinkle with smoked paprika, salt, and pepper.
7. Roast chickpeas in the preheated oven for 20-25 minutes, or until crispy.
8. Once the soup is cooked, use an immersion blender to blend until smooth. Alternatively, transfer the soup to a blender and blend until smooth, then return to the pot.
9. Season with salt and pepper to taste.
10. Serve the cauliflower and potato soup hot, topped with crispy chickpeas and fresh parsley if desired.
11. Enjoy this creamy and flavorful soup with a crunchy twist!

Nutritional Info (per serving): Calories: 220 Fat: 6g Carbs: 35g Protein: 8g

Vegetable Noodle Soup with Plant-Based Meatballs

Prep: 20 mins | Cook: 30 mins | Serves: 4

Ingredients:

- For the Plant-Based Meatballs:
- 1 cup cooked lentils
- 1/2 cup breadcrumbs
- 1/4 cup chopped onion
- 2 cloves garlic, minced
- 1 tbsp tomato paste
- 1 tsp Italian seasoning
- Salt and pepper to taste
- Olive oil for frying

  For the Soup:
1. 1 tbsp olive oil
2. 1 onion, diced
3. 2 carrots, diced
4. 2 celery stalks, diced
5. 2 cloves garlic, minced
6. 6 cups vegetable broth
7. 2 cups cooked noodles (such as spaghetti or fettuccine)
8. Salt and pepper to taste
9. Fresh parsley for garnish (optional)

Instructions:

1. To make the plant-based meatballs, combine cooked lentils, breadcrumbs, chopped onion, minced garlic, tomato paste, Italian seasoning, salt, and pepper in a bowl. Mix until well combined.
2. Shape the mixture into small balls.
3. Heat olive oil in a skillet over medium heat. Fry the meatballs until golden brown on all sides. Set aside.
4. In a large pot, heat olive oil over medium heat.
5. Add diced onion, carrots, and celery. Cook until softened, about 5 minutes.
6. Stir in minced garlic and cook for another 2 minutes.
7. Pour in vegetable broth and bring to a boil.
8. Add cooked noodles and plant-based meatballs to the pot. Simmer for 10 minutes.
9. Season with salt and pepper to taste.
10. Serve the vegetable noodle soup hot, garnished with fresh parsley if desired.

11. Enjoy this comforting and satisfying soup with hearty plant-based meatballs!

Nutritional Info (per serving): Calories: 280 Fat: 8g Carbs: 40g Protein: 12g

Black Bean and Quinoa Chili

Prep: 15 mins | Cook: 40 mins | Serves: 6

Ingredients:

- 1 tbsp olive oil
- 1 onion, diced
- 2 cloves garlic, minced
- 1 bell pepper, diced
- 1 zucchini, diced
- 1 cup cooked quinoa
- 2 cans (15 oz each) black beans, drained and rinsed (US) / 400g canned black beans, drained and rinsed (UK)
- 1 can (14 oz) diced tomatoes (US) / 400g canned diced tomatoes (UK)
- 2 cups vegetable broth
- 2 tbsp chili powder
- 1 tsp ground cumin
- Salt and pepper to taste
- Fresh cilantro for garnish (optional)
- Avocado slices for serving (optional)

Instructions:

1. Heat olive oil in a large pot over medium heat.
2. Add diced onion and minced garlic. Cook until softened, about 5 minutes.
3. Stir in diced bell pepper and zucchini. Cook for another 5 minutes.
4. Add cooked quinoa, black beans, diced tomatoes, vegetable broth, chili powder, and ground cumin. Stir to combine.
5. Bring the chili to a simmer, then reduce heat to low and cover. Let it simmer for 30 minutes, stirring occasionally.
6. Season with salt and pepper to taste.
7. Serve the black bean and quinoa chili hot, garnished with fresh cilantro and avocado slices if desired.
8. Enjoy this protein-packed and flavorful chili!

Nutritional Info (per serving): Calories: 280 Fat: 6g Carbs: 45g Protein: 10g

Roasted Red Pepper and Tomato Soup with Basil

Prep: 15 mins | Cook: 40 mins | Serves: 4

Ingredients:

- 2 red bell peppers
- 4 tomatoes
- 2 tbsp olive oil
- 1 onion, diced
- 2 cloves garlic, minced
- 4 cups vegetable broth
- 1/4 cup chopped fresh basil
- Salt and pepper to taste
- Balsamic glaze for drizzling (optional)
- Croutons for serving (optional)

Instructions:

1. Preheat the oven to 400°F (200°C).
2. Place red bell peppers and tomatoes on a baking sheet lined with parchment paper. Drizzle with olive oil and season with salt and pepper.
3. Roast in the preheated oven for 25-30 minutes, or until vegetables are softened and slightly charred.
4. Remove from the oven and let cool slightly. Peel and seed the red bell peppers.
5. In a large pot, heat olive oil over medium heat.
6. Add diced onion and minced garlic. Cook until softened, about 5 minutes.
7. Add roasted red bell peppers, tomatoes, and vegetable broth to the pot. Bring to a simmer.
8. Stir in chopped fresh basil. Cook for another 10 minutes.
9. Using an immersion blender, blend the soup until smooth. Alternatively, transfer the soup to a blender and blend until smooth, then return to the pot.
10. Season with salt and pepper to taste.
11. Serve the roasted red pepper and tomato soup hot, drizzled with balsamic glaze and topped with croutons if desired.
12. Enjoy this rich and comforting soup with a hint of sweetness from the roasted peppers!

Nutritional Info (per serving): Calories: 180 Fat: 8g Carbs: 25g rotein: 4g

Creamy Vegetable Soup with Cashew Cream

Prep: 15 mins | Cook: 30 mins | Serves: 4

Ingredients:

- 1 tbsp olive oil
- 1 onion, diced
- 2 cloves garlic, minced
- 2 carrots, diced
- 2 celery stalks, diced
- 1 potato, peeled and diced
- 4 cups vegetable broth
- 1 cup cauliflower florets
- 1/2 cup raw cashews, soaked in water for 2 hours
- Salt and pepper to taste
- Fresh parsley for garnish (optional)

Instructions:

1. Heat olive oil in a large pot over medium heat.
2. Add diced onion and minced garlic. Cook until softened, about 5 minutes.
3. Stir in diced carrots, celery, and potato. Cook for another 5 minutes.
4. Pour in vegetable broth and bring to a boil.
5. Add cauliflower florets to the pot. Simmer for 15 minutes, or until vegetables are tender.
6. In a blender, combine soaked cashews with 1 cup of water. Blend until smooth to make cashew cream.
7. Add cashew cream to the soup and stir to combine. Simmer for another 5 minutes.
8. Season with salt and pepper to taste.
9. Serve the creamy vegetable soup hot, garnished with fresh parsley if desired.
10. Enjoy this velvety and indulgent soup that's dairy-free and packed with flavor!

Nutritional Info (per serving): Calories: 220 Fat: 12g Carbs: 25g Protein: 6g

Split Pea and Vegetable Soup

Prep: 15 mins | Cook: 1 hour | Serves: 6

Ingredients:

- 1 tbsp olive oil
- 1 onion, diced
- 2 cloves garlic, minced

- 2 carrots, diced
- 2 celery stalks, diced
- 1 potato, peeled and diced
- 2 cups split peas, rinsed
- 6 cups vegetable broth
- 1 bay leaf
- Salt and pepper to taste
- Lemon wedges for serving (optional)

Instructions:

1. Heat olive oil in a large pot over medium heat.
2. Add diced onion and minced garlic. Cook until softened, about 5 minutes.
3. Stir in diced carrots, celery, and potato. Cook for another 5 minutes.
4. Add split peas, vegetable broth, and bay leaf to the pot. Bring to a boil.
5. Reduce heat to low and cover. Let the soup simmer for 45-60 minutes, or until split peas are tender and soup has thickened.
6. Remove the bay leaf and discard.
7. Season with salt and pepper to taste.
8. Serve the split pea and vegetable soup hot, with lemon wedges on the side for squeezing.
9. Enjoy this comforting and hearty soup that's perfect for chilly days!

Nutritional Info (per serving): Calories: 250 Fat: 3g Carbs: 45g Protein: 14g

Vegan Corn Chowder with Smoky Tempeh Bacon

Prep: 15 mins | Cook: 30 mins | Serves: 4

Ingredients:

- 2 tbsp olive oil
- 1 onion, diced
- 2 cloves garlic, minced
- 2 potatoes, peeled and diced
- 2 cups corn kernels (fresh or frozen)
- 4 cups vegetable broth
- 1 cup unsweetened almond milk
- 1/4 cup nutritional yeast
- Salt and pepper to taste
- Smoked paprika for seasoning
- Tempeh bacon for garnish (optional)

- Chopped chives for garnish (optional)

Instructions:

1. Heat olive oil in a large pot over medium heat.
2. Add diced onion and minced garlic. Cook until softened, about 5 minutes.
3. Stir in diced potatoes and corn kernels. Cook for another 5 minutes.
4. Pour in vegetable broth and bring to a boil.
5. Reduce heat to low and cover. Let the soup simmer for 15-20 minutes, or until potatoes are tender.
6. Using an immersion blender, blend part of the soup to desired consistency, leaving some chunks for texture.
7. Stir in unsweetened almond milk and nutritional yeast. Season with salt, pepper, and smoked paprika to taste.
8. Cook for another 5 minutes, allowing flavors to meld.
9. Serve the vegan corn chowder hot, garnished with smoky tempeh bacon and chopped chives if desired.
10. Enjoy this creamy and flavorful chowder that's perfect for any occasion!

Nutritional Info (per serving): Calories: 280 Fat: 10g Carbs: 40g Protein: 10g

Carrot and Ginger Soup with Coconut Milk

Prep: 15 mins | Cook: 30 mins | Serves: 4

Ingredients:

- 2 tbsp coconut oil
- 1 onion, diced
- 2 cloves garlic, minced
- 1 lb carrots, peeled and diced
- 1-inch piece of ginger, grated
- 4 cups vegetable broth
- 1 can (14 oz) coconut milk (US) / 400ml coconut milk (UK)
- 1 tbsp maple syrup or honey
- Salt and pepper to taste
- Fresh cilantro for garnish (optional)

Instructions:

1. Heat coconut oil in a large pot over medium heat.
2. Add diced onion and minced garlic. Cook until softened, about 5 minutes.
3. Stir in diced carrots and grated ginger. Cook for another 5 minutes.

4. Pour in vegetable broth and bring to a boil.
5. Reduce heat to low and cover. Let the soup simmer for 20-25 minutes, or until carrots are tender.
6. Using an immersion blender, blend the soup until smooth.
7. Stir in coconut milk and maple syrup or honey. Season with salt and pepper to taste.
8. Cook for another 5 minutes, allowing flavors to meld.
9. Serve the carrot and ginger soup hot, garnished with fresh cilantro if desired.
10. Enjoy this vibrant and aromatic soup that's both comforting and nutritious!

Nutritional Info (per serving): Calories: 220 Fat: 15g Carbs: 20g Protein: 3g

Vegetable and Tofu Miso Soup

Prep: 10 mins | Cook: 20 mins | Serves: 4

Ingredients:

- 4 cups vegetable broth
- 1 block (14 oz) firm tofu, diced (US) / 400g firm tofu, diced (UK)
- 1 cup sliced mushrooms
- 2 green onions, sliced
- 2 tbsp miso paste
- 1 cup chopped spinach
- 1 sheet nori, cut into thin strips
- 1 tsp sesame oil
- 1 tbsp soy sauce
- Fresh cilantro for garnish (optional)

Instructions:

1. In a large pot, bring vegetable broth to a simmer over medium heat.
2. Add diced tofu, sliced mushrooms, and sliced green onions to the pot. Simmer for 10 minutes.
3. In a small bowl, mix miso paste with a few tablespoons of hot broth until dissolved.
4. Add the miso mixture to the pot and stir well to combine.
5. Stir in chopped spinach and nori strips. Cook for another 5 minutes.
6. Add sesame oil and soy sauce to the soup. Adjust seasoning if necessary.
7. Serve the vegetable and tofu miso soup hot, garnished with fresh cilantro if desired.
8. Enjoy this comforting and nourishing soup that's packed with umami flavor!

Nutritional Info (per serving): Calories: 180 Fat: 10g Carbs: 10g Protein: 15g

MAIN DISHES: GRAINS, LEGUMES, AND VEGETABLES

Quinoa and Roasted Vegetable Bowls

Prep: 15 mins | Cook: 30 mins | Serves: 4

Ingredients:

- 1 cup quinoa, rinsed
- 2 cups mixed vegetables (such as bell peppers, zucchini, and cherry tomatoes), chopped
- 2 tbsp olive oil
- Salt and pepper to taste
- 1 avocado, sliced
- 1/4 cup hummus
- Fresh parsley for garnish (optional)

Instructions:

1. Preheat the oven to 400°F (200°C).
2. Cook quinoa according to package instructions.
3. On a baking sheet, toss mixed vegetables with olive oil, salt, and pepper.
4. Roast in the preheated oven for 20-25 minutes, or until vegetables are tender and slightly caramelized.
5. Divide cooked quinoa among serving bowls.
6. Top with roasted vegetables, sliced avocado, and a dollop of hummus.
7. Garnish with fresh parsley if desired.
8. Serve the quinoa and roasted vegetable bowls hot and enjoy this nutritious and flavorful meal!

Nutritional Info (per serving): Calories: 350 Fat: 15g Carbs: 45g Protein: 10g

Lentil and Vegetable Curry with Coconut Milk

Prep: 20 mins | Cook: 40 mins | Serves: 6

Ingredients:

- 1 cup dried lentils
- 2 cups mixed vegetables (such as carrots, potatoes, and peas), diced
- 1 onion, diced
- 2 cloves garlic, minced
- 1 can (14 oz) coconut milk (US) / 400ml coconut milk (UK)
- 2 tbsp curry powder

- 1 tsp ground turmeric
- Salt and pepper to taste
- Fresh cilantro for garnish (optional)

Instructions:

1. Rinse lentils under cold water and drain.
2. In a large pot, heat olive oil over medium heat.
3. Add diced onion and minced garlic. Cook until softened, about 5 minutes.
4. Stir in curry powder and ground turmeric. Cook for another 2 minutes.
5. Add lentils, mixed vegetables, and coconut milk to the pot. Stir to combine.
6. Bring to a boil, then reduce heat to low and cover. Let it simmer for 30 minutes, or until lentils and vegetables are tender.
7. Season with salt and pepper to taste.
8. Serve the lentil and vegetable curry hot, garnished with fresh cilantro if desired.
9. Enjoy this hearty and comforting curry with basmati rice or naan bread!

Nutritional Info (per serving): Calories: 320 Fat: 15g Carbs: 35g Protein: 12g

Baked Sweet Potatoes with Black Bean Chili

Prep: 15 mins | Cook: 1 hour | Serves: 4

Ingredients:

- 4 medium sweet potatoes
- 1 can (14 oz) black beans, drained and rinsed (US) / 400g canned black beans, drained and rinsed (UK)
- 1 onion, diced
- 2 cloves garlic, minced
- 1 bell pepper, diced
- 1 cup corn kernels (fresh or frozen)
- 1 can (14 oz) diced tomatoes (US) / 400g canned diced tomatoes (UK)
- 1 tbsp chili powder
- 1 tsp ground cumin
- Salt and pepper to taste
- Fresh cilantro for garnish (optional)
- Lime wedges for serving (optional)

Instructions:

1. Preheat the oven to 400°F (200°C).
2. Scrub sweet potatoes clean and pierce them with a fork several times.

3. Place sweet potatoes on a baking sheet lined with parchment paper. Bake in the preheated oven for 45-60 minutes, or until tender.
4. While sweet potatoes are baking, prepare the black bean chili.
5. In a large skillet, heat olive oil over medium heat.
6. Add diced onion and minced garlic. Cook until softened, about 5 minutes.
7. Stir in diced bell pepper, corn kernels, black beans, diced tomatoes, chili powder, and ground cumin. Cook for another 10 minutes, stirring occasionally.
8. Season with salt and pepper to taste.
9. Once sweet potatoes are baked, slice them open and fluff the flesh with a fork.
10. Spoon black bean chili over each baked sweet potato.
11. Garnish with fresh cilantro and serve with lime wedges if desired.
12. Enjoy these flavorful baked sweet potatoes with hearty black bean chili!

Nutritional Info (per serving): Calories: 350 Fat: 2g Carbs: 75g Protein: 12g

Whole Grain Pasta with Marinara Sauce and Roasted Veggies

Prep: 15 mins | Cook: 30 mins | Serves: 4

Ingredients:

- 8 oz whole grain pasta
- 2 cups mixed vegetables (such as cherry tomatoes, broccoli, and bell peppers), chopped
- 2 tbsp olive oil
- Salt and pepper to taste
- 2 cups marinara sauce (store-bought or homemade)
- Fresh basil for garnish (optional)
- Grated plant-based cheese for serving (optional)

Instructions:

1. Cook whole grain pasta according to package instructions. Drain and set aside.
2. Preheat the oven to 400°F (200°C).
3. Toss mixed vegetables with olive oil, salt, and pepper on a baking sheet lined with parchment paper.
4. Roast in the preheated oven for 20-25 minutes, or until vegetables are tender and slightly charred.
5. In a large skillet, heat marinara sauce over medium heat until warmed through.
6. Add cooked pasta to the skillet with marinara sauce and toss to coat.
7. Divide pasta among serving plates and top with roasted vegetables.
8. Garnish with fresh basil and sprinkle with grated plant-based cheese if desired.

9. Serve the whole grain pasta with marinara sauce and roasted veggies hot.
10. Enjoy this wholesome and satisfying pasta dish that's packed with flavor and nutrients!

Nutritional Info (per serving): Calories: 350 Fat: 8g Carbs: 60g Protein: 12g

Vegetable Stir-Fry with Brown Rice or Quinoa

Prep: 15 mins | Cook: 15 mins | Serves: 4

Ingredients:

- 2 cups mixed vegetables (such as broccoli, bell peppers, carrots, and snap peas), chopped
- 1 onion, sliced
- 2 cloves garlic, minced
- 1 tbsp olive oil
- 1/4 cup low-sodium soy sauce (US) / 60ml low-sodium soy sauce (UK)
- 2 tbsp rice vinegar
- 1 tbsp maple syrup or honey
- 1 tsp sesame oil
- 2 cups cooked brown rice or quinoa
- Sesame seeds for garnish (optional)
- Sliced green onions for garnish (optional)

Instructions:

1. Heat olive oil in a large skillet or wok over medium-high heat.
2. Add sliced onion and minced garlic. Stir-fry for 2-3 minutes until fragrant.
3. Add mixed vegetables to the skillet. Stir-fry for another 5-7 minutes until vegetables are tender but still crisp.
4. In a small bowl, whisk together low-sodium soy sauce, rice vinegar, maple syrup or honey, and sesame oil.
5. Pour the sauce over the vegetables in the skillet. Stir well to coat.
6. Cook for another 2-3 minutes until the sauce thickens slightly.
7. Serve the vegetable stir-fry hot over cooked brown rice or quinoa.
8. Garnish with sesame seeds and sliced green onions if desired.
9. Enjoy this flavorful and nutritious vegetable stir-fry as a delicious main dish!

Nutritional Info (per serving, without rice/quinoa): Calories: 100 Fat: 4g Carbs: 15g Protein: 5g

Stuffed Bell Peppers with Rice and Plant-Based Protein

Prep: 20 mins | Cook: 40 mins | Serves: 4

Ingredients:

- 4 bell peppers, halved and seeds removed
- 1 cup cooked brown rice
- 1 can (14 oz) black beans, drained and rinsed (US) / 400g canned black beans, drained and rinsed (UK)
- 1 cup corn kernels (fresh or frozen)
- 1 onion, diced
- 2 cloves garlic, minced
- 1 tsp ground cumin
- 1 tsp chili powder
- Salt and pepper to taste
- Plant-based cheese for topping (optional)
- Fresh cilantro for garnish (optional)

Instructions:

1. Preheat the oven to 375°F (190°C).
2. In a large skillet, heat olive oil over medium heat.
3. Add diced onion and minced garlic. Cook until softened, about 5 minutes.
4. Stir in cooked brown rice, black beans, corn kernels, ground cumin, chili powder, salt, and pepper. Cook for another 5 minutes, until heated through.
5. Place bell pepper halves in a baking dish, cut side up.
6. Spoon the rice and bean mixture into each bell pepper half, pressing down gently.
7. Cover the baking dish with foil and bake in the preheated oven for 30 minutes.
8. Remove foil and sprinkle plant-based cheese on top of each stuffed bell pepper, if using.
9. Return to the oven and bake for an additional 10 minutes, or until the cheese is melted and bubbly.
10. Serve the stuffed bell peppers hot, garnished with fresh cilantro if desired.
11. Enjoy these hearty and flavorful stuffed bell peppers as a satisfying main dish!

Nutritional Info (per serving): Calories: 250 Fat: 3g Carbs: 45g Protein: 10g

Vegetable and Tofu Pad Thai with Rice Noodles

Prep: 20 mins | Cook: 15 mins | Serves: 4

Ingredients:

- 8 oz rice noodles
- 1 block (14 oz) firm tofu, drained and pressed (US) / 400g firm tofu, drained and pressed (UK)
- 2 cups mixed vegetables (such as bell peppers, bean sprouts, and carrots), sliced
- 3 cloves garlic, minced
- 2 green onions, sliced
- 1/4 cup peanuts, chopped (optional)
- 2 tbsp vegetable oil
- 3 tbsp soy sauce
- 2 tbsp tamarind paste
- 2 tbsp maple syrup or brown sugar
- 1 tbsp rice vinegar
- 1 tsp chili flakes (optional)
- Lime wedges for serving (optional)
- Fresh cilantro for garnish (optional)

Instructions:

1. Cook rice noodles according to package instructions. Drain and set aside.
2. Cut pressed tofu into cubes.
3. Heat vegetable oil in a large skillet or wok over medium-high heat.
4. Add tofu cubes to the skillet and cook until golden brown on all sides, about 5-7 minutes. Remove tofu from the skillet and set aside.
5. In the same skillet, add minced garlic and sliced green onions. Cook for 1-2 minutes until fragrant.
6. Add sliced mixed vegetables to the skillet and stir-fry for 3-5 minutes until tender-crisp.
7. In a small bowl, whisk together soy sauce, tamarind paste, maple syrup or brown sugar, rice vinegar, and chili flakes if using.
8. Add cooked rice noodles, cooked tofu, and the sauce mixture to the skillet. Toss everything together until well combined and heated through.
9. Serve the vegetable and tofu pad thai hot, garnished with chopped peanuts, lime wedges, and fresh cilantro if desired.
10. Enjoy this delicious and satisfying pad thai dish packed with flavor and texture!

Nutritional Info (per serving): Calories: 400 Fat: 15g Carbs: 55g Protein: 15g

Lentil and Vegetable Shepherd's Pie

Prep: 20 mins | Cook: 40 mins | Serves: 6

Ingredients:

- 1 cup dried green or brown lentils
- 2 cups vegetable broth
- 2 tbsp olive oil
- 1 onion, diced
- 2 carrots, diced
- 2 celery stalks, diced
- 2 cloves garlic, minced
- 1 cup frozen peas
- 1 cup frozen corn kernels
- 2 tbsp tomato paste
- 1 tbsp soy sauce
- 1 tsp dried thyme
- Mashed potatoes for topping (store-bought or homemade)
- Fresh parsley for garnish (optional)

Instructions:

1. Rinse lentils under cold water and drain.
2. In a medium pot, combine lentils and vegetable broth. Bring to a boil, then reduce heat to low and simmer for 20-25 minutes, or until lentils are tender and most of the liquid is absorbed. Drain any excess liquid and set aside.
3. Preheat the oven to 375°F (190°C).
4. In a large skillet, heat olive oil over medium heat.
5. Add diced onion, carrots, and celery. Cook until softened, about 5-7 minutes.
6. Add minced garlic, frozen peas, and frozen corn kernels to the skillet. Cook for another 2-3 minutes.
7. Stir in cooked lentils, tomato paste, soy sauce, and dried thyme. Cook for 2-3 minutes until heated through and well combined.
8. Transfer the lentil and vegetable mixture to a baking dish.
9. Spread mashed potatoes evenly over the top of the lentil mixture.
10. Bake in the preheated oven for 20-25 minutes, or until the mashed potatoes are golden brown and the filling is bubbly.
11. Serve the lentil and vegetable shepherd's pie hot, garnished with fresh parsley if desired.
12. Enjoy this comforting and hearty shepherd's pie that's perfect for a cozy meal!

Nutritional Info (per serving): Calories: 350 Fat: 10g Carbs: 55g Protein: 15g

Veggie Burgers with Sweet Potato Fries

Prep: 20 mins | Cook: 30 mins | Serves: 4

Ingredients:

- For Veggie Burgers:
- 1 can (14 oz) black beans, drained and rinsed (US) / 400g canned black beans, drained and rinsed (UK)
- 1 cup cooked quinoa
- 1/2 cup breadcrumbs
- 1 onion, finely chopped
- 2 cloves garlic, minced
- 1 tsp ground cumin
- 1 tsp chili powder
- Salt and pepper to taste
- 1 tbsp olive oil
- **For Sweet Potato Fries:**
- 2 large sweet potatoes, cut into fries
- 2 tbsp olive oil
- 1 tsp paprika
- 1/2 tsp garlic powder
- Salt and pepper to taste
- **For Serving:**
- Burger buns
- Lettuce, tomato slices, avocado slices, etc. (optional)
- Ketchup, mustard, vegan mayo, etc. (optional)

Instructions:

1. 1 Preheat the oven to 425°F (220°C) and line a baking sheet with parchment paper.
2. In a large bowl, mash black beans with a fork until mostly smooth but still a bit chunky.
3. Add cooked quinoa, breadcrumbs, chopped onion, minced garlic, ground cumin, chili powder, salt, and pepper to the bowl. Mix well to combine.
4. Divide the mixture into four equal portions and shape each portion into a burger patty.
5. Heat olive oil in a skillet over medium heat. Cook the veggie burgers for 4-5 minutes on each side, or until golden brown and heated through.
6. While the burgers are cooking, prepare the sweet potato fries.
7. In a separate bowl, toss sweet potato fries with olive oil, paprika, garlic powder, salt, and pepper until evenly coated.

8. Spread the sweet potato fries in a single layer on the prepared baking sheet.
9. Bake in the preheated oven for 25-30 minutes, flipping halfway through, until crispy and golden brown.
10. Assemble the veggie burgers by placing each cooked patty on a bun and topping with lettuce, tomato slices, avocado slices, or any other desired toppings.
11. Serve with sweet potato fries and condiments of your choice.
12. Enjoy these homemade veggie burgers with crispy sweet potato fries for a delicious and satisfying meal!

Nutritional Info (per serving, including fries but without toppings): Calories: 450 Fat: 15g Carbs: 65g Protein: 15g

Baked Falafel with Tahini Sauce and Salad

Prep: 20 mins | Cook: 25 mins | Serves: 4

Ingredients:

- For Baked Falafel:
- 1 can (14 oz) chickpeas, drained and rinsed (US) / 400g canned chickpeas, drained and rinsed (UK)
- 1/2 cup fresh parsley, chopped
- 1/4 cup fresh cilantro, chopped
- 1 small onion, chopped
- 2 cloves garlic, minced
- 1 tsp ground cumin
- 1 tsp ground coriander
- 1/2 tsp baking powder
- Salt and pepper to taste
- 2 tbsp olive oil
  For Tahini Sauce:
- 1/4 cup tahini
- 2 tbsp lemon juice
- 1 clove garlic, minced
- Water, as needed
- Salt to taste
  For Salad:
- Mixed greens
- Cherry tomatoes, halved
- Cucumber, sliced
- Red onion, thinly sliced

- Kalamata olives (optional)

Instructions:

1. 1 Preheat the oven to 375°F (190°C) and line a baking sheet with parchment paper.
2. In a food processor, combine chickpeas, parsley, cilantro, onion, garlic, ground cumin, ground coriander, baking powder, salt, and pepper. Pulse until well combined but still slightly chunky.
3. With wet hands, shape the mixture into small patties and place them on the prepared baking sheet.
4. Drizzle olive oil over the falafel patties.
5. Bake in the preheated oven for 20-25 minutes, flipping halfway through, until golden brown and crispy.
6. While the falafel is baking, prepare the tahini sauce. In a small bowl, whisk together tahini, lemon juice, minced garlic, and a splash of water until smooth and creamy. Add more water as needed to reach desired consistency. Season with salt to taste.
7. Assemble the salad by tossing mixed greens, cherry tomatoes, cucumber slices, red onion slices, and kalamata olives if using.
8. Serve the baked falafel hot with tahini sauce drizzled on top, alongside the prepared salad.
9. Enjoy these flavorful baked falafel with creamy tahini sauce and a refreshing salad for a satisfying meal!

Nutritional Info (per serving, including tahini sauce but without salad): Calories: 300 Fat: 18g Carbs: 25g Protein: 10g

Grilled Portobello Mushroom Caps with Quinoa and Roasted Vegetables

Prep: 20 mins | Cook: 25 mins | Serves: 4

Ingredients:

- For Grilled Portobello Mushroom Caps:
- 4 large portobello mushroom caps
- 2 tbsp balsamic vinegar
- 2 cloves garlic, minced
- 2 tbsp olive oil
- Salt and pepper to taste
  For Quinoa:
- 1 cup quinoa, rinsed
- 2 cups vegetable broth
- 1 tbsp olive oil

- Salt to taste

For Roasted Vegetables:
- 2 cups mixed vegetables (such as bell peppers, zucchini, and eggplant), chopped
- 1 tbsp olive oil
- Salt and pepper to taste
- 1 tsp Italian seasoning

Instructions:

1. 1 Preheat the grill to medium-high heat.
2. In a small bowl, whisk together balsamic vinegar, minced garlic, olive oil, salt, and pepper.
3. Brush both sides of the portobello mushroom caps with the balsamic mixture.
4. Grill the mushroom caps for 4-5 minutes on each side, or until tender and grill marks appear. Remove from the grill and set aside.
5. In a medium pot, combine quinoa and vegetable broth. Bring to a boil, then reduce heat to low and simmer for 15 minutes, or until quinoa is cooked and liquid is absorbed. Fluff with a fork and set aside.
6. Preheat the oven to 400°F (200°C).
7. On a baking sheet, toss mixed vegetables with olive oil, salt, pepper, and Italian seasoning.
8. Roast in the preheated oven for 15-20 minutes, or until vegetables are tender and slightly caramelized.
9. To serve, divide cooked quinoa among plates. Top with grilled portobello mushroom caps and roasted vegetables.
10. Enjoy this hearty and nutritious meal of grilled portobello mushroom caps with quinoa and roasted vegetables!

Nutritional Info (per serving): Calories: 300 Fat: 10g Carbs: 45g Protein: 12g

Vegetable and Tofu Stir-Fry with Rice Noodles

Prep: 15 mins | Cook: 15 mins | Serves: 4

Ingredients:

- 8 oz rice noodles
- 1 block (14 oz) firm tofu, drained and pressed (US) / 400g firm tofu, drained and pressed (UK)
- 2 cups mixed vegetables (such as broccoli, bell peppers, and snap peas), sliced
- 3 cloves garlic, minced
- 2 tbsp soy sauce

- 1 tbsp hoisin sauce
- 1 tbsp sesame oil
- 1 tsp cornstarch
- 2 tbsp water
- 2 green onions, sliced
- Sesame seeds for garnish (optional)

Instructions:

1. Cook rice noodles according to package instructions. Drain and set aside.
2. Cut pressed tofu into cubes.
3. In a small bowl, whisk together soy sauce, hoisin sauce, sesame oil, cornstarch, and water to make the sauce. Set aside.
4. Heat olive oil in a large skillet or wok over medium-high heat.
5. Add tofu cubes to the skillet and cook until golden brown on all sides, about 5-7 minutes. Remove tofu from the skillet and set aside.
6. In the same skillet, add minced garlic and sliced mixed vegetables. Stir-fry for 3-5 minutes until vegetables are tender-crisp.
7. Return cooked tofu to the skillet and pour the sauce over the tofu and vegetables.
8. Stir well to coat everything in the sauce and cook for another 2-3 minutes until heated through and sauce has thickened.
9. Add cooked rice noodles to the skillet and toss to combine with the tofu and vegetables.
10. Garnish with sliced green onions and sesame seeds if desired.
11. Serve the vegetable and tofu stir-fry hot and enjoy this delicious and satisfying dish!

Nutritional Info (per serving): Calories: 350 Fat: 10g Carbs: 50g Protein: 15g

Black Bean and Sweet Potato Enchiladas

Prep: 20 mins | Cook: 30 mins | Serves: 4

Ingredients:

- 8 corn tortillas
- 1 can (14 oz) black beans, drained and rinsed (US) / 400g canned black beans, drained and rinsed (UK)
- 2 cups sweet potatoes, peeled and diced
- 1 onion, diced
- 2 cloves garlic, minced
- 1 bell pepper, diced
- 1 cup corn kernels (fresh or frozen)

- 1 cup enchilada sauce (store-bought or homemade)
- 1 cup shredded plant-based cheese
- 1 tbsp olive oil
- Salt and pepper to taste
- Fresh cilantro for garnish (optional)
- Sliced avocado for serving (optional)

Instructions:

a. 1 Preheat the oven to 375°F (190°C).
b. 2. Heat olive oil in a large skillet over medium heat.
c. 3. Add diced onion and minced garlic. Cook until softened, about 5 minutes.
5. Add diced sweet potatoes to the skillet and cook for 8-10 minutes, or until tender.
6. Stir in diced bell pepper and corn kernels. Cook for another 2-3 minutes.
7. Add black beans to the skillet and season with salt and pepper to taste. Cook for 2-3 minutes until heated through.
8. Spread a thin layer of enchilada sauce on the bottom of a baking dish.
9. Warm corn tortillas in the microwave for 30 seconds to make them pliable.
10. Spoon the sweet potato and black bean mixture onto each tortilla, roll them up, and place them seam side down in the baking dish.
11. Pour the remaining enchilada sauce over the rolled tortillas.
12. Sprinkle shredded plant-based cheese over the top of the enchiladas.
13. Cover the baking dish with foil and bake in the preheated oven for 20-25 minutes, or until heated through and cheese is melted.
14. Remove foil and bake for an additional 5 minutes to brown the cheese slightly.
15. Serve the black bean and sweet potato enchiladas hot, garnished with fresh cilantro and sliced avocado if desired.
16. Enjoy these flavorful and satisfying enchiladas as a delicious main dish!

Nutritional Info (per serving): Calories: 400 Fat: 15g Carbs: 55g Protein: 15g

Cauliflower and Chickpea Curry with Basmati Rice

Prep: 15 mins | Cook: 30 mins | Serves: 4

Ingredients:

- 1 head cauliflower, cut into florets
- 1 can (14 oz) chickpeas, drained and rinsed (US) / 400g canned chickpeas, drained and rinsed (UK)
- 1 onion, diced
- 2 cloves garlic, minced

- 1-inch piece ginger, grated
- 1 can (14 oz) diced tomatoes (US) / 400g canned diced tomatoes (UK)
- 1 can (14 oz) coconut milk
- 2 tbsp curry powder
- 1 tsp ground turmeric
- 1 tsp ground cumin
- Salt and pepper to taste
- 2 tbsp olive oil
- Fresh cilantro for garnish (optional)
- Cooked basmati rice for serving

Instructions:

1. Heat olive oil in a large skillet or pot over medium heat.
2. Add diced onion, minced garlic, and grated ginger. Cook until softened and fragrant, about 5 minutes.
3. Stir in curry powder, ground turmeric, and ground cumin. Cook for another minute until spices are toasted and fragrant.
4. Add cauliflower florets to the skillet and cook for 5 minutes, stirring occasionally.
5. Add diced tomatoes, chickpeas, and coconut milk to the skillet. Stir to combine.
6. Bring the mixture to a simmer, then reduce heat to low and cover. Let it simmer for 15-20 minutes, or until cauliflower is tender.
7. Season with salt and pepper to taste.
8. Serve the cauliflower and chickpea curry hot over cooked basmati rice.
9. Garnish with fresh cilantro if desired.
10. Enjoy this flavorful and comforting curry as a satisfying meal!

Nutritional Info (per serving, without rice): Calories: 300 Fat: 15g Carbs: 35g Protein: 10g

Vegetable Lasagna with Plant-Based Cheese

Prep: 30 mins | Cook: 45 mins | Serves: 6

Ingredients:

- 9 lasagna noodles
- 2 cups marinara sauce (store-bought or homemade)
- 2 cups mixed vegetables (such as zucchini, bell peppers, and mushrooms), sliced
- 1 onion, diced
- 2 cloves garlic, minced
- 2 cups spinach leaves
- 1 cup plant-based ricotta cheese

- 1 cup shredded plant-based mozzarella cheese
- 1/4 cup nutritional yeast
- 1 tbsp olive oil
- Salt and pepper to taste
- Fresh basil for garnish (optional)

Instructions:

1. 1 Preheat the oven to 375°F (190°C) and lightly grease a 9x13-inch baking dish.
2. Cook lasagna noodles according to package instructions. Drain and set aside.
3. Heat olive oil in a large skillet over medium heat.
4. Add diced onion and minced garlic. Cook until softened, about 5 minutes.
5. Add sliced mixed vegetables to the skillet. Cook for 5-7 minutes until tender.
6. Stir in spinach leaves and cook until wilted. Season with salt and pepper to taste.
7. In a mixing bowl, combine plant-based ricotta cheese and nutritional yeast. Mix well.
8. To assemble the lasagna, spread a thin layer of marinara sauce on the bottom of the prepared baking dish.
9. Place three lasagna noodles on top of the sauce.
10. Spread half of the vegetable mixture over the noodles.
11. Dollop half of the plant-based ricotta cheese mixture over the vegetables.
12. Sprinkle half of the shredded plant-based mozzarella cheese over the ricotta cheese layer.
13. Repeat the layers with marinara sauce, lasagna noodles, remaining vegetable mixture, remaining ricotta cheese mixture, and remaining shredded mozzarella cheese.
14. Cover the baking dish with foil and bake in the preheated oven for 30 minutes.
15. Remove foil and bake for an additional 15 minutes, or until cheese is bubbly and golden brown.
16. Let the vegetable lasagna cool for a few minutes before slicing.
17. Garnish with fresh basil leaves if desired.
18. Serve hot and enjoy this comforting and flavorful vegetable lasagna!

Nutritional Info (per serving): Calories: 350 Fat: 10g Carbs: 45g Protein: 15g

MAIN DISHES: PLANT-BASED PROTEINS

Tofu Stir-Fry with Broccoli and Cashews

Prep: 15 mins | Cook: 15 mins | Serves: 4

Ingredients:

- 1 block (14 oz) firm tofu, drained and pressed (US) / 400g firm tofu, drained and pressed (UK)
- 2 cups broccoli florets
- 1/2 cup cashews
- 1 onion, sliced
- 2 cloves garlic, minced
- 1 red bell pepper, sliced
- 2 tbsp soy sauce
- 1 tbsp sesame oil
- 1 tbsp rice vinegar
- 1 tsp cornstarch
- Cooked brown rice for serving

Instructions:

a. 1 Cut pressed tofu into cubes.
b. 2. Heat sesame oil in a large skillet or wok over medium-high heat.
c. 3. Add tofu cubes to the skillet and cook until golden brown on all sides, about 5-7 minutes. Remove tofu from the skillet and set aside.
5. In the same skillet, add sliced onion, minced garlic, and broccoli florets. Stir-fry for 3-4 minutes until broccoli is tender-crisp.
6. Return cooked tofu to the skillet and add sliced red bell pepper.
7. In a small bowl, whisk together soy sauce, rice vinegar, and cornstarch. Pour the sauce over the tofu and vegetables in the skillet.
8. Stir well to coat everything in the sauce and cook for another 2-3 minutes until heated through and sauce has thickened.
9. Toss in cashews and cook for an additional minute.
10. Serve the tofu stir-fry hot over cooked brown rice.
11. Enjoy this flavorful and nutritious tofu dish!

Nutritional Info (per serving, without rice): Calories: 300 Fat: 20g Carbs: 15g Protein: 18g

Lentil and Vegetable Meatballs with Marinara Sauce

Prep: 20 mins | Cook: 30 mins | Serves: 4

Ingredients:

- 1 cup dried lentils
- 2 cups vegetable broth
- 1 onion, finely chopped
- 2 cloves garlic, minced
- 1 carrot, grated
- 1 zucchini, grated
- 1/4 cup breadcrumbs
- 2 tbsp nutritional yeast
- 1 tsp dried oregano
- 1 tsp dried basil
- Salt and pepper to taste
- 2 cups marinara sauce (store-bought or homemade)
- Cooked spaghetti for serving

Instructions:

1. In a medium pot, combine dried lentils and vegetable broth. Bring to a boil, then reduce heat to low and simmer for 20-25 minutes, or until lentils are tender and most of the liquid is absorbed.
2. Preheat the oven to 375°F (190°C) and lightly grease a baking sheet.
3. In a large bowl, mash cooked lentils with a fork or potato masher until they form a paste-like consistency.
4. Add finely chopped onion, minced garlic, grated carrot, grated zucchini, breadcrumbs, nutritional yeast, dried oregano, dried basil, salt, and pepper to the bowl. Mix well to combine.
5. Shape the lentil mixture into golf ball-sized meatballs and place them on the prepared baking sheet.
6. Bake in the preheated oven for 20-25 minutes, or until meatballs are firm and slightly golden brown.
7. While the meatballs are baking, heat marinara sauce in a large skillet over medium heat.
8. Once the meatballs are cooked, transfer them to the skillet with the marinara sauce.
9. Gently toss the meatballs in the sauce until evenly coated.
10. Serve the lentil and vegetable meatballs hot over cooked spaghetti.

11. Enjoy this delicious and satisfying plant-based alternative to traditional meatballs!

Nutritional Info (per serving, without spaghetti): Calories: 250 Fat: 5g Carbs: 35g Protein: 15g

Grilled Tempeh Kebabs with Pineapple and Bell Peppers

Prep: 20 mins | Cook: 15 mins | Serves: 4

Ingredients:

- 2 packages (16 oz total) tempeh, cut into cubes
- 1 large pineapple, peeled, cored, and cut into chunks
- 2 bell peppers (any color), cut into chunks
- 1 red onion, cut into chunks
- 1/4 cup soy sauce
- 2 tbsp maple syrup
- 2 tbsp olive oil
- 2 cloves garlic, minced
- 1 tsp ground ginger
- Salt and pepper to taste
- Wooden skewers, soaked in water for 30 minutes

Instructions:

1. In a small bowl, whisk together soy sauce, maple syrup, olive oil, minced garlic, ground ginger, salt, and pepper to make the marinade.
2. Place tempeh cubes in a shallow dish and pour the marinade over them. Let marinate for at least 15 minutes, or up to 1 hour in the refrigerator.
3. Preheat the grill to medium-high heat.
4. Thread marinated tempeh cubes, pineapple chunks, bell pepper chunks, and red onion chunks onto the soaked wooden skewers, alternating the ingredients.
5. Brush the grill grates with oil to prevent sticking.
6. Grill the kebabs for 10-15 minutes, turning occasionally, until the tempeh is lightly charred and the vegetables are tender.
7. Remove the kebabs from the grill and serve hot.
8. Enjoy these flavorful and nutritious grilled tempeh kebabs with pineapple and bell peppers as a delicious main dish!

Nutritional Info (per serving): Calories: 300 Fat: 12g Carbs: 30g Protein: 20g

Chickpea and Spinach Curry with Coconut Milk

Prep: 15 mins | Cook: 25 mins | Serves: 4

Ingredients:

- 2 cans (14 oz each) chickpeas, drained and rinsed (US) / 400g canned chickpeas, drained and rinsed (UK)
- 1 onion, finely chopped
- 2 cloves garlic, minced
- 1-inch piece ginger, grated
- 1 can (14 oz) diced tomatoes (US) / 400g canned diced tomatoes (UK)
- 1 can (14 oz) coconut milk
- 2 cups spinach leaves
- 2 tbsp curry powder
- 1 tsp ground turmeric
- 1 tsp ground cumin
- 1 tbsp olive oil
- Salt and pepper to taste
- Cooked rice for serving

Instructions:

1. Heat olive oil in a large skillet or pot over medium heat.
2. Add finely chopped onion, minced garlic, and grated ginger. Cook until softened and fragrant, about 5 minutes.
3. Stir in curry powder, ground turmeric, and ground cumin. Cook for another minute until spices are toasted and fragrant.
4. Add diced tomatoes, drained chickpeas, and coconut milk to the skillet. Stir to combine.
5. Bring the mixture to a simmer, then reduce heat to low and cover. Let it simmer for 15-20 minutes, stirring occasionally.
6. Stir in spinach leaves and cook until wilted.
7. Season with salt and pepper to taste.
8. Serve the chickpea and spinach curry hot over cooked rice.
9. Enjoy this flavorful and comforting curry as a satisfying meal!

Nutritional Info (per serving, without rice): Calories: 350 Fat: 20g Carbs: 35g Protein: 15g

Vegetable and Tofu Stir-Fry with Peanut Sauce

Prep: 15 mins | Cook: 15 mins | Serves: 4

Ingredients:

- 1 block (14 oz) firm tofu, drained and pressed (US) / 400g firm tofu, drained and pressed (UK)
- 2 cups mixed vegetables (such as broccoli, bell peppers, and snap peas), sliced
- 1 onion, sliced
- 2 cloves garlic, minced
- 1/4 cup peanuts, chopped
- Cooked rice or noodles for serving

  For Peanut Sauce:
- 1/4 cup peanut butter
- 2 tbsp soy sauce
- 1 tbsp maple syrup
- 1 tbsp rice vinegar
- 1 clove garlic, minced
- 1 tsp grated ginger
- 2-3 tbsp water, as needed to thin the sauce

Instructions:

1. Cut pressed tofu into cubes.
2. Heat olive oil in a large skillet or wok over medium-high heat.
3. Add tofu cubes to the skillet and cook until golden brown on all sides, about 5-7 minutes. Remove tofu from the skillet and set aside.
4. In the same skillet, add sliced onion, minced garlic, and mixed vegetables. Stir-fry for 3-4 minutes until vegetables are tender-crisp.
5. While the vegetables are cooking, prepare the peanut sauce. In a small bowl, whisk together peanut butter, soy sauce, maple syrup, rice vinegar, minced garlic, and grated ginger. Add water gradually until desired consistency is reached.
6. Return cooked tofu to the skillet with the vegetables.
7. Pour the peanut sauce over the tofu and vegetables in the skillet.
8. Stir well to coat everything in the sauce and cook for another 2-3 minutes until heated through.
9. Serve the vegetable and tofu stir-fry hot over cooked rice or noodles.
10. Garnish with chopped peanuts.

11. Enjoy this delicious and flavorful stir-fry with peanut sauce!

Nutritional Info (per serving, without rice or noodles): Calories: 300 Fat: 20g Carbs: 15g Protein: 18g

Baked Tofu with Teriyaki Glaze and Steamed Vegetables

Prep: 10 mins | Cook: 25 mins | Serves: 4

Ingredients:

- 1 block (14 oz) firm tofu, drained and pressed (US) / 400g firm tofu, drained and pressed (UK)
- 1 cup teriyaki sauce (store-bought or homemade)
- 2 cups mixed vegetables (such as broccoli, carrots, and snow peas)
- Cooked rice for serving

Instructions:

1. Preheat the oven to 375°F (190°C).
2. Cut pressed tofu into slices or cubes.
3. Place tofu in a shallow dish and pour teriyaki sauce over it. Let marinate for at least 15 minutes.
4. Transfer marinated tofu to a baking dish lined with parchment paper or lightly greased.
5. Bake tofu in the preheated oven for 20-25 minutes, flipping halfway through, until tofu is golden brown and slightly crispy.
6. While the tofu is baking, steam mixed vegetables until tender.
7. Serve baked tofu hot over cooked rice, with steamed vegetables on the side.
8. Enjoy this flavorful and satisfying dish of baked tofu with teriyaki glaze and steamed vegetables!

Nutritional Info (per serving, without rice): Calories: 250 Fat: 10g Carbs: 20g Protein: 15g

Lentil and Walnut Loaf with Mushroom Gravy

Prep: 20 mins | Cook: 1 hour | Serves: 6

Ingredients for Lentil and Walnut Loaf:

- 1 cup dried green lentils
- 2 cups vegetable broth
- 1 onion, finely chopped
- 2 cloves garlic, minced
- 1 carrot, grated
- 1/2 cup walnuts, chopped

- 1/4 cup breadcrumbs
- 2 tbsp tomato paste
- 1 tbsp soy sauce
- 1 tsp dried thyme
- 1 tsp dried rosemary
- Salt and pepper to taste

Ingredients for Mushroom Gravy:

- 2 cups mushrooms, sliced
- 1 onion, finely chopped
- 2 cloves garlic, minced
- 2 cups vegetable broth
- 2 tbsp all-purpose flour
- 2 tbsp olive oil
- 1 tsp soy sauce
- Salt and pepper to taste

Instructions for Lentil and Walnut Loaf:

1. Preheat the oven to 375°F (190°C) and lightly grease a loaf pan.
2. Rinse dried lentils under cold water and drain.
3. In a medium pot, combine dried lentils and vegetable broth. Bring to a boil, then reduce heat to low and simmer for 20-25 minutes, or until lentils are tender and most of the liquid is absorbed.
4. In a large bowl, mash cooked lentils with a fork or potato masher until they form a paste-like consistency.
5. Add finely chopped onion, minced garlic, grated carrot, chopped walnuts, breadcrumbs, tomato paste, soy sauce, dried thyme, dried rosemary, salt, and pepper to the bowl. Mix well to combine.
6. Transfer the lentil mixture to the prepared loaf pan and press it down evenly.
7. Bake in the preheated oven for 40-45 minutes, or until the top is golden brown and firm to the touch.
8. Let the lentil loaf cool for a few minutes before slicing.

Instructions for Mushroom Gravy:

1. Heat olive oil in a large skillet over medium heat.
2. Add finely chopped onion and minced garlic. Cook until softened and fragrant, about 5 minutes.

3. Add sliced mushrooms to the skillet and cook until they release their juices and become tender, about 5-7 minutes.
4. Sprinkle flour over the mushrooms and stir to combine, cooking for another minute.
5. Gradually whisk in vegetable broth, stirring constantly to prevent lumps from forming.
6. Bring the gravy to a simmer, then reduce heat to low and let it thicken for 5-7 minutes, stirring occasionally.
7. Stir in soy sauce, salt, and pepper to taste.
8. Serve the lentil and walnut loaf slices with mushroom gravy poured over the top.
9. Enjoy this hearty and flavorful lentil loaf with mushroom gravy as a satisfying main dish!

Nutritional Info (per serving, loaf only): Calories: 300 Fat: 10g Carbs: 40g Protein: 15g

Nutritional Info (per serving, gravy only): Calories: 50 Fat: 3g Carbs: 5g Protein: 2g

Seitan Fajitas with Grilled Vegetables and Guacamole

Prep: 20 mins | Cook: 20 mins | Serves: 4

Ingredients for Seitan Fajitas:

- 1 package (8 oz) seitan, sliced into strips
- 2 bell peppers (any color), sliced
- 1 onion, sliced
- 1 tbsp olive oil
- 1 tsp chili powder
- 1/2 tsp cumin
- 1/2 tsp smoked paprika
- Salt and pepper to taste
- 8 small flour tortillas

Ingredients for Guacamole:

- 2 ripe avocados
- 1 tomato, diced
- 1/4 cup red onion, finely chopped
- 1/4 cup cilantro, chopped
- 1 lime, juiced
- Salt and pepper to taste

Instructions for Seitan Fajitas:

1. Heat olive oil in a large skillet over medium-high heat.

2. Add sliced bell peppers and onion to the skillet. Cook until they start to soften, about 5 minutes.
3. Push the vegetables to one side of the skillet and add seitan strips to the other side.
4. Season the seitan with chili powder, cumin, smoked paprika, salt, and pepper. Cook until seitan is heated through and slightly browned, about 5-7 minutes.
5. Once everything is cooked, mix the seitan with the vegetables in the skillet.
6. Warm flour tortillas in a dry skillet or microwave according to package instructions.
7. Serve seitan and vegetable mixture on warm tortillas.
8. Top with guacamole and any additional toppings of your choice.
9. Enjoy these flavorful seitan fajitas with grilled vegetables and guacamole as a delicious and satisfying meal!

Instructions for Guacamole:

1. 1 Cut avocados in half, remove pits, and scoop flesh into a bowl.
2. Mash avocado with a fork until desired consistency is reached.
3. Add diced tomato, finely chopped red onion, chopped cilantro, lime juice, salt, and pepper to the bowl.
4. Mix everything together until well combined.
5. Taste and adjust seasoning if needed.
6. Serve guacamole immediately or cover and refrigerate until ready to use.
7. Enjoy this fresh and creamy guacamole with your seitan fajitas!

Nutritional Info (per serving, fajitas only): Calories: 300 Fat: 10g Carbs: 35g Protein: 15g

Nutritional Info (per serving, guacamole only): Calories: 100 Fat: 8g Carbs: 6g Protein: 2g

Tempeh and Vegetable Stir-Fry with Brown Rice

Prep: 15 mins | Cook: 20 mins | Serves: 4

Ingredients:

- 1 package (8 oz) tempeh, sliced into strips
- 2 cups mixed vegetables (such as broccoli, carrots, and bell peppers), sliced
- 1 onion, sliced
- 2 cloves garlic, minced
- 2 tbsp soy sauce
- 1 tbsp maple syrup
- 1 tbsp rice vinegar
- 1 tbsp sesame oil
- Cooked brown rice for serving

Instructions:

1. Heat sesame oil in a large skillet or wok over medium-high heat.
2. Add sliced tempeh to the skillet and cook until golden brown on all sides, about 5-7 minutes. Remove tempeh from the skillet and set aside.
3. In the same skillet, add sliced onion and minced garlic. Cook until softened and fragrant, about 3-4 minutes.
4. Add mixed vegetables to the skillet and stir-fry for 5-7 minutes until tender-crisp.
5. In a small bowl, whisk together soy sauce, maple syrup, and rice vinegar. Pour the sauce over the vegetables in the skillet.
6. Return cooked tempeh to the skillet and stir well to coat everything in the sauce.
7. Cook for another 2-3 minutes until heated through.
8. Serve the tempeh and vegetable stir-fry hot over cooked brown rice.
9. Enjoy this delicious and nutritious stir-fry as a satisfying meal!

Nutritional Info (per serving, without rice): Calories: 250 Fat: 10g Carbs: 20g Protein: 15g

Chickpea and Vegetable Burgers with Sweet Potato Fries

Prep: 20 mins | Cook: 30 mins | Serves: 4

Ingredients for Chickpea and Vegetable Burgers:

- 1 can (14 oz) chickpeas, drained and rinsed (US) / 400g canned chickpeas, drained and rinsed (UK)
- 1 cup cooked quinoa
- 1 carrot, grated
- 1/2 onion, finely chopped
- 2 cloves garlic, minced
- 1/4 cup breadcrumbs
- 2 tbsp nutritional yeast
- 1 tsp ground cumin
- 1/2 tsp smoked paprika
- Salt and pepper to taste
- 4 whole grain burger buns

Ingredients for Sweet Potato Fries:

- 2 large sweet potatoes, cut into fries
- 2 tbsp olive oil
- 1 tsp garlic powder
- 1 tsp paprika
- Salt and pepper to taste

Instructions for Chickpea and Vegetable Burgers:

1. 1 Preheat the oven to 375°F (190°C) and line a baking sheet with parchment paper.
2. In a large bowl, mash chickpeas with a fork or potato masher until slightly chunky.
3. Add cooked quinoa, grated carrot, finely chopped onion, minced garlic, breadcrumbs, nutritional yeast, ground cumin, smoked paprika, salt, and pepper to the bowl. Mix until well combined.
4. Divide the mixture into 4 equal portions and shape each portion into a patty.
5. Place the patties on the prepared baking sheet and bake in the preheated oven for 25-30 minutes, flipping halfway through, until golden brown and crispy.
6. While the burgers are baking, prepare the sweet potato fries.

Instructions for Sweet Potato Fries:

1. 1 Increase the oven temperature to 400°F (200°C).
2. Place sweet potato fries on a baking sheet lined with parchment paper.
3. Drizzle olive oil over the fries and sprinkle with garlic powder, paprika, salt, and pepper. Toss to coat evenly.
4. Spread the fries out in a single layer on the baking sheet.
5. Bake in the preheated oven for 20-25 minutes, flipping halfway through, until fries are crispy and golden brown.

Nutritional Info (per serving, burgers only): Calories: 300 Fat: 8g Carbs: 45gProtein: 12g

Nutritional Info (per serving, fries only): Calories: 150 Fat: 6g Carbs: 25g Protein: 2g

Tofu and Vegetable Sushi Rolls with Pickled Ginger

Prep: 30 mins | Cook: 20 mins | Serves: 4

Ingredients for Tofu and Vegetable Sushi Rolls:

- 1 cup sushi rice
- 2 cups water
- 4 nori seaweed sheets
- 1 block (14 oz) firm tofu, sliced into strips
- 1 avocado, sliced
- 1 cucumber, julienned
- 1 carrot, julienned
- Pickled ginger, for serving
- Soy sauce and wasabi, for dipping

For Sushi Rice Seasoning:

- 2 tbsp rice vinegar

- 1 tbsp sugar
- 1/2 tsp salt

Instructions:

1. 1 Rinse sushi rice under cold water until the water runs clear. Drain well.
2. In a medium saucepan, combine sushi rice and water. Bring to a boil, then reduce heat to low, cover, and simmer for 18-20 minutes, or until rice is tender and water is absorbed.
3. In a small bowl, mix rice vinegar, sugar, and salt until sugar and salt are dissolved.
4. Transfer cooked rice to a large bowl and gently fold in the sushi rice seasoning until well combined. Let the rice cool to room temperature.
5. Place a nori seaweed sheet shiny side down on a bamboo sushi mat or a clean kitchen towel.
6. Spread a thin layer of sushi rice evenly over the nori, leaving about 1 inch of space at the top edge.
7. Arrange tofu strips, avocado slices, cucumber, and carrot in a line across the center of the rice.
8. Starting from the bottom edge, tightly roll up the sushi using the bamboo mat or kitchen towel, pressing gently as you roll to seal the edge.
9. Once rolled, use a sharp knife to slice the sushi roll into 6-8 pieces.
10. Repeat with the remaining nori sheets and fillings.
11. Serve sushi rolls with pickled ginger, soy sauce, and wasabi for dipping.
12. Enjoy these delicious tofu and vegetable sushi rolls as a nutritious and satisfying meal!

Nutritional Info (per serving, sushi rolls only): Calories: 250 Fat: 5g Carbs: 45g Protein: 10g

Tempeh and Vegetable Fried Rice

Prep: 15 mins | Cook: 20 mins | Serves: 4

Ingredients:

- 1 cup cooked brown rice
- 1 package (8 oz) tempeh, crumbled
- 2 cups mixed vegetables (such as peas, carrots, and corn)
- 1 onion, chopped
- 2 cloves garlic, minced
- 2 tbsp soy sauce
- 1 tbsp sesame oil
- 1 tbsp rice vinegar
- 1 tsp grated ginger

- 2 green onions, chopped (for garnish)
- Sesame seeds (for garnish)

Instructions:

1. Heat sesame oil in a large skillet or wok over medium heat.
2. Add chopped onion and minced garlic to the skillet. Cook until softened and fragrant, about 3-4 minutes.
3. Add crumbled tempeh to the skillet. Cook until golden brown and slightly crispy, about 5-7 minutes.
4. Add mixed vegetables to the skillet. Cook until tender, about 5 minutes.
5. Stir in cooked brown rice, soy sauce, rice vinegar, and grated ginger. Cook for another 3-5 minutes, stirring constantly, until everything is heated through and well combined.
6. Taste and adjust seasoning if needed.
7. Serve tempeh and vegetable fried rice hot, garnished with chopped green onions and sesame seeds.
8. Enjoy this flavorful and nutritious fried rice as a delicious main dish!

Nutritional Info (per serving): Calories: 300 Fat: 10g Carbs: 35g Protein: 15g

Baked Seitan with BBQ Sauce and Roasted Vegetables

Prep: 15 mins | Cook: 30 mins | Serves: 4

Ingredients for Baked Seitan:

- 1 package (8 oz) seitan, sliced into strips
- 1/2 cup barbecue sauce (store-bought or homemade)

Ingredients for Roasted Vegetables:

- 2 cups mixed vegetables (such as bell peppers, zucchini, and onions), sliced
- 2 tbsp olive oil
- 1 tsp dried thyme
- 1 tsp dried rosemary
- Salt and pepper to taste

Instructions for Baked Seitan:

1. Preheat the oven to 375°F (190°C) and line a baking sheet with parchment paper.
2. Place seitan strips on the prepared baking sheet.
3. Brush both sides of seitan strips with barbecue sauce.
4. Bake in the preheated oven for 20-25 minutes, flipping halfway through, until seitan is heated through and slightly caramelized.

Instructions for Roasted Vegetables:

1. Preheat the oven to 400°F (200°C) and line a baking sheet with parchment paper.
2. In a large bowl, toss sliced mixed vegetables with olive oil, dried thyme, dried rosemary, salt, and pepper until well coated.
3. Spread the vegetables out in a single layer on the prepared baking sheet.
4. Roast in the preheated oven for 20-25 minutes, stirring halfway through, until vegetables are tender and slightly caramelized.

Nutritional Info (per serving, seitan only): Calories: 200 Fat: 2g Carbs: 15g Protein: 25g

Nutritional Info (per serving, vegetables only): Calories: 100 Fat: 6g Carbs: 12g Protein: 2g

Chickpea and Spinach Stew with Whole Grain Pita

Prep: 15 mins | Cook: 25 mins | Serves: 4

Ingredients for Chickpea and Spinach Stew:

- 2 cans (15 oz each) chickpeas, drained and rinsed (US) / 400g canned chickpeas, drained and rinsed (UK)
- 1 onion, chopped
- 2 cloves garlic, minced
- 1 can (14 oz) diced tomatoes (US) / 400g canned diced tomatoes (UK)
- 4 cups fresh spinach leaves
- 2 cups vegetable broth
- 1 tsp ground cumin
- 1 tsp paprika
- Salt and pepper to taste
- Fresh lemon wedges, for serving

Ingredients for Whole Grain Pita:

- 4 whole grain pitas

Instructions for Chickpea and Spinach Stew:

1. Heat olive oil in a large pot over medium heat.
2. Add chopped onion and minced garlic to the pot. Cook until softened and fragrant, about 3-4 minutes.
3. Add ground cumin and paprika to the pot. Cook for another minute, stirring constantly.
4. Stir in diced tomatoes and vegetable broth. Bring to a simmer.
5. Add drained and rinsed chickpeas to the pot. Simmer for 15-20 minutes, allowing the flavors to meld and the stew to thicken slightly.
6. Stir in fresh spinach leaves and cook until wilted, about 2-3 minutes.

7. Taste and adjust seasoning with salt and pepper as needed.
8. Serve the chickpea and spinach stew hot, with fresh lemon wedges on the side.

Instructions for Whole Grain Pita:

1. Preheat oven to 350°F (175°C).
2. Place whole grain pitas on a baking sheet.
3. Bake in the preheated oven for 5-7 minutes, or until pitas are warmed through.

Nutritional Info (per serving, stew only): Calories: 250 Fat: 4g Carbs: 45g Protein: 12g

Nutritional Info (per serving, pita only): Calories: 150 Fat: 1g Carbs: 30g Protein: 5g

Tofu and Vegetable Pad Thai with Rice Noodles

Prep: 20 mins | Cook: 15 mins | Serves: 4

Ingredients for Tofu and Vegetable Pad Thai:

- 8 oz rice noodles
- 1 block (14 oz) firm tofu, pressed and cubed
- 2 cups mixed vegetables (such as bell peppers, carrots, and broccoli), sliced
- 3 green onions, chopped
- 2 cloves garlic, minced
- 2 tbsp soy sauce
- 2 tbsp tamarind paste
- 1 tbsp maple syrup
- 1 tbsp rice vinegar
- 1 tbsp vegetable oil
- Crushed peanuts, for garnish
- Fresh cilantro, for garnish
- Lime wedges, for serving

Instructions:

1. Cook rice noodles according to package instructions. Drain and set aside.
2. In a small bowl, whisk together soy sauce, tamarind paste, maple syrup, and rice vinegar to make the sauce.
3. Heat vegetable oil in a large skillet or wok over medium-high heat.
4. Add cubed tofu to the skillet and cook until golden brown on all sides, about 5-7 minutes. Remove tofu from the skillet and set aside.
5. In the same skillet, add sliced mixed vegetables and minced garlic. Stir-fry for 3-4 minutes until vegetables are tender-crisp.
6. Add cooked rice noodles and tofu back to the skillet.

7. Pour the sauce over the noodles and tofu. Toss everything together until well coated in the sauce.
8. Cook for another 2-3 minutes, stirring constantly, until heated through.
9. Remove from heat and stir in chopped green onions.
10. Serve tofu and vegetable pad Thai hot, garnished with crushed peanuts, fresh cilantro, and lime wedges.

Nutritional Info (per serving): Calories: 350 Fat: 10g Carbs: 55g Protein: 15g

SNACKS AND SIDES

Roasted Chickpeas with Spices

Prep: 10 mins | Cook: 30 mins | Serves: 4

Ingredients:

- 2 cans (15 oz each) chickpeas, drained and rinsed (US) / 400g canned chickpeas, drained and rinsed (UK)
- 2 tbsp olive oil
- 1 tsp ground cumin
- 1 tsp paprika
- 1/2 tsp garlic powder
- Salt and pepper to taste

Instructions:

1. Preheat the oven to 400°F (200°C) and line a baking sheet with parchment paper.
2. Pat dry the chickpeas with paper towels to remove excess moisture.
3. In a bowl, toss the chickpeas with olive oil, ground cumin, paprika, garlic powder, salt, and pepper until evenly coated.
4. Spread the seasoned chickpeas out on the prepared baking sheet in a single layer.
5. Roast in the preheated oven for 25-30 minutes, stirring halfway through, until crispy and golden brown.
6. Remove from the oven and let cool slightly before serving.
7. Enjoy these crunchy and flavorful roasted chickpeas as a nutritious snack!

Nutritional Info (per serving): Calories: 200 Fat: 8g Carbs: 25g Protein: 8g

Baked Sweet Potato Fries with Avocado Dipping Sauce

Prep: 15 mins | Cook: 25 mins | Serves: 4

- Ingredients for Sweet Potato Fries:
- 2 large sweet potatoes, cut into fries
- 2 tbsp olive oil
- 1 tsp garlic powder
- 1 tsp paprika
- Salt and pepper to taste

Ingredients for Avocado Dipping Sauce:

- 1 ripe avocado
- 1/4 cup Greek yogurt (or dairy-free alternative)
- 1 tbsp lime juice
- 1 clove garlic, minced
- Salt and pepper to taste

Instructions for Sweet Potato Fries:

1. Preheat the oven to 425°F (220°C) and line a baking sheet with parchment paper.
2. In a large bowl, toss sweet potato fries with olive oil, garlic powder, paprika, salt, and pepper until evenly coated.
3. Spread the seasoned sweet potato fries out on the prepared baking sheet in a single layer.
4. Bake in the preheated oven for 20-25 minutes, flipping halfway through, until fries are crispy and golden brown.

Instructions for Avocado Dipping Sauce:

1. In a small bowl, mash the avocado until smooth.
2. Stir in Greek yogurt, lime juice, minced garlic, salt, and pepper until well combined.
3. Adjust seasoning to taste, adding more lime juice or salt if desired.
4. Serve the baked sweet potato fries with the avocado dipping sauce on the side.
5. Enjoy these delicious and nutritious sweet potato fries with creamy avocado sauce as a satisfying snack or side dish!

Nutritional Info (per serving, fries only): Calories: 150 Fat: 6g Carbs: 25g Protein: 2g

Nutritional Info (per serving, sauce only): Calories: 50 Fat: 4g Carbs: 3g Protein: 1g

Kale Chips with Nutritional Yeast

Prep: 10 mins | Cook: 20 mins | Serves: 4

Ingredients:

- 1 bunch kale, stems removed and leaves torn into bite-sized pieces
- 1 tbsp olive oil
- 2 tbsp nutritional yeast
- 1/2 tsp garlic powder
- Salt to taste

Instructions:

1. Preheat the oven to 350°F (175°C) and line a baking sheet with parchment paper.

2. In a large bowl, toss kale leaves with olive oil until evenly coated.
3. Sprinkle nutritional yeast, garlic powder, and salt over the kale leaves, tossing to coat evenly.
4. Spread the seasoned kale leaves out on the prepared baking sheet in a single layer.
5. Bake in the preheated oven for 15-20 minutes, or until kale is crispy and slightly browned around the edges.
6. Remove from the oven and let cool slightly before serving.
7. Enjoy these crispy and flavorful kale chips as a healthy snack or side dish!

Nutritional Info (per serving): Calories: 50 Fat: 3g Carbs: 5g Protein: 3g

Hummus and Veggie Wraps with Whole Grain Tortillas

Prep: 10 mins | Cook: 0 mins | Serves: 4

Ingredients:

- 4 whole grain tortillas
- 1 cup hummus (store-bought or homemade)
- 2 cups mixed vegetables (such as lettuce, cucumber, bell peppers, and carrots), thinly sliced

Instructions:

1. Lay a tortilla flat on a clean surface.
2. Spread a generous layer of hummus evenly over the tortilla.
3. Arrange mixed vegetables in a line down the center of the tortilla.
4. Fold in the sides of the tortilla, then roll it up tightly from the bottom to form a wrap.
5. Repeat with the remaining tortillas and ingredients.
6. Slice each wrap in half diagonally, if desired.
7. Serve hummus and veggie wraps immediately, or wrap tightly in foil or parchment paper for later.

Nutritional Info (per serving): Calories: 200 Fat: 6g Carbs: 30g Protein: 8g

Avocado Toast with Tomato and Basil

Prep: 5 mins | Cook: 5 mins | Serves: 2

Ingredients:

- 2 slices whole grain bread
- 1 ripe avocado
- 1 tomato, sliced
- Fresh basil leaves

- Salt and pepper to taste
- Red pepper flakes (optional)

Instructions:

1. Toast the slices of whole grain bread until golden brown.
2. While the bread is toasting, halve and pit the avocado. Scoop the flesh into a bowl and mash it with a fork until smooth.
3. Spread mashed avocado evenly onto each slice of toasted bread.
4. Top the avocado toast with sliced tomato and fresh basil leaves.
5. Season with salt, pepper, and red pepper flakes, if desired.
6. Serve immediately and enjoy this simple yet delicious avocado toast!

Nutritional Info (per serving): Calories: 200 Fat: 10g Carbs: 20g Protein: 6g

Edamame with Sea Salt

Prep: 5 mins | Cook: 5 mins | Serves: 2

Ingredients:

- 1 cup edamame (frozen or fresh)
- Sea salt to taste

Instructions:

1. If using frozen edamame, thaw according to package instructions. If using fresh edamame, shell them.
2. Bring a pot of water to a boil and add the edamame.
3. Cook for 3-5 minutes, or until the edamame are tender.
4. Drain the edamame and transfer them to a serving bowl.
5. Sprinkle with sea salt to taste.
6. Toss to coat evenly and serve immediately.
7. Enjoy these nutritious and protein-packed edamame as a satisfying snack or side dish!

Nutritional Info (per serving): Calories: 100 Fat: 3g Carbs: 10g Protein: 8g

Fruit Skewers with Yogurt Dipping Sauce

Prep: 15 mins | Cook: 0 mins | Serves: 4

Ingredients:

- Assorted fruits (such as strawberries, pineapple, grapes, and melon), chopped into bite-sized pieces
- Wooden skewers

Ingredients for Yogurt Dipping Sauce:

- 1 cup Greek yogurt (or dairy-free alternative)
- 1 tbsp honey (or maple syrup)
- 1 tsp vanilla extract

Instructions:

1. Thread the assorted fruit pieces onto wooden skewers, alternating between different fruits.
2. In a small bowl, whisk together Greek yogurt, honey, and vanilla extract until smooth.
3. Serve fruit skewers with yogurt dipping sauce on the side.
4. Enjoy these colorful and refreshing fruit skewers with creamy yogurt dipping sauce as a healthy snack or dessert!

Nutritional Info (per serving, fruit skewers only): Calories: 80 Fat: 0g Carbs: 20g Protein: 1g

Nutritional Info (per serving, yogurt dipping sauce only): Calories: 60 Fat: 0g Carbs: 10g Protein: 6g

Baked Apple Chips with Cinnamon

Prep: 10 mins | Cook: 2 hours | Serves: 4

Ingredients:

- 2 large apples
- 1 tbsp lemon juice
- 1 tsp ground cinnamon

Instructions:

1. Preheat the oven to 200°F (95°C) and line a baking sheet with parchment paper.
2. Core the apples and thinly slice them crosswise into rounds, about 1/8 inch thick.
3. In a large bowl, toss the apple slices with lemon juice to prevent browning.
4. Arrange the apple slices in a single layer on the prepared baking sheet.
5. Sprinkle ground cinnamon evenly over the apple slices.
6. Bake in the preheated oven for 1.5 to 2 hours, or until the apple chips are dried and slightly crispy.
7. Remove from the oven and let cool completely before serving.
8. Enjoy these crunchy and naturally sweet baked apple chips as a wholesome snack!

Nutritional Info (per serving): Calories: 50 Fat: 0g Carbs: 15g Protein: 0g

Veggie and Tofu Spring Rolls with Peanut Dipping Sauce

Prep: 20 mins | Cook: 0 mins | Serves: 4

Ingredients for Spring Rolls:

- 8 rice paper wrappers
- 1 block (14 oz) firm tofu, sliced into thin strips
- 2 cups mixed vegetables (such as carrots, cucumber, bell peppers, and lettuce), julienned
- Fresh mint leaves
- Fresh cilantro leaves

Ingredients for Peanut Dipping Sauce:

- 1/4 cup peanut butter
- 2 tbsp soy sauce
- 1 tbsp rice vinegar
- 1 tbsp honey (or maple syrup)
- 1 clove garlic, minced
- Water (as needed to thin out the sauce)

Instructions for Spring Rolls:

1. Prepare all the vegetables and tofu for the spring rolls and set aside.
2. Fill a shallow dish with warm water. Dip one rice paper wrapper into the water for a few seconds until it becomes pliable.
3. Lay the damp rice paper wrapper flat on a clean surface.
4. Place a few slices of tofu and a handful of mixed vegetables in the center of the wrapper.
5. Add fresh mint and cilantro leaves on top of the vegetables.
6. Fold the bottom edge of the wrapper over the filling, then fold in the sides, and roll tightly to seal.
7. Repeat with the remaining wrappers and filling ingredients.

Instructions for Peanut Dipping Sauce:

1. In a small bowl, whisk together peanut butter, soy sauce, rice vinegar, honey, and minced garlic until smooth.
2. If the sauce is too thick, add water, a tablespoon at a time, until desired consistency is reached.
3. Adjust seasoning to taste, adding more soy sauce or honey if needed.

Nutritional Info (per serving, spring rolls only): Calories: 200 Fat: 4g Carbs: 35g Protein: 8g

Nutritional Info (per serving, peanut dipping sauce only): Calories: 80 Fat: 6g Carbs: 5g Protein: 3g

Cucumber and Carrot Sticks with Tzatziki Sauce

Prep: 10 mins | Cook: 0 mins | Serves: 4

Ingredients for Tzatziki Sauce:

- 1 cup Greek yogurt (or dairy-free alternative)
- 1 cucumber, grated and squeezed to remove excess moisture
- 1 clove garlic, minced
- 1 tbsp fresh dill, chopped
- 1 tbsp lemon juice
- Salt and pepper to taste

Instructions for Tzatziki Sauce:

1. In a bowl, combine Greek yogurt, grated cucumber, minced garlic, chopped dill, and lemon juice.
2. Stir until well combined.
3. Season with salt and pepper to taste.
4. Cover and refrigerate for at least 30 minutes to allow the flavors to meld.

Nutritional Info (per serving, tzatziki sauce only): Calories: 60 Fat: 0g Carbs: 7g Protein: 8g

Roasted Beet and Orange Salad with Walnuts

Prep: 15 mins | Cook: 45 mins | Serves: 4

Ingredients:

- 4 medium beets, peeled and cubed
- 2 oranges, peeled and sliced
- 1/4 cup walnuts, chopped
- 4 cups mixed greens
- 2 tbsp olive oil
- 1 tbsp balsamic vinegar
- Salt and pepper to taste

Instructions:

1. Preheat the oven to 400°F (200°C) and line a baking sheet with parchment paper.
2. Place the cubed beets on the prepared baking sheet and drizzle with olive oil. Season with salt and pepper to taste.

3. Roast the beets in the preheated oven for 40-45 minutes, or until tender and caramelized.
4. In a small bowl, whisk together olive oil and balsamic vinegar to make the dressing.
5. In a large serving bowl, combine mixed greens, roasted beets, and orange slices.
6. Drizzle the dressing over the salad and toss gently to coat.
7. Sprinkle chopped walnuts over the salad just before serving.
8. Enjoy this vibrant and flavorful roasted beet and orange salad as a nutritious side dish or light meal!

Nutritional Info (per serving): Calories: 180 Fat: 10g Carbs: 20g Protein: 4g

Quinoa and Black Bean Stuffed Avocados

Prep: 15 mins | Cook: 15 mins | Serves: 4

Ingredients:

- 2 ripe avocados
- 1 cup cooked quinoa
- 1 cup black beans, drained and rinsed
- 1/2 cup cherry tomatoes, halved
- 1/4 cup red onion, finely chopped
- 2 tbsp fresh cilantro, chopped
- 1 lime, juiced
- Salt and pepper to taste

Instructions:

1. Cut the avocados in half and remove the pits. Scoop out a little extra flesh from each avocado half to create a larger cavity.
2. In a bowl, combine cooked quinoa, black beans, cherry tomatoes, red onion, cilantro, and lime juice. Season with salt and pepper to taste.
3. Spoon the quinoa and black bean mixture into the avocado halves, dividing it evenly among them.
4. Serve immediately and enjoy these nutritious and satisfying quinoa and black bean stuffed avocados as a wholesome meal or appetizer!

Nutritional Info (per serving): Calories: 250 Fat: 15g Carbs: 25g Protein: 7g

Baked Zucchini Fries with Marinara Sauce

Prep: 15 mins | Cook: 20 mins | Serves: 4

Ingredients:

- 2 large zucchinis
- 1/2 cup breadcrumbs
- 1/4 cup grated Parmesan cheese (optional)
- 1 tsp garlic powder
- 1 tsp dried oregano
- Salt and pepper to taste
- Cooking spray
- Marinara sauce for dipping

Instructions:

1. Preheat the oven to 425°F (220°C) and line a baking sheet with parchment paper.
2. Cut the zucchinis into fry-shaped sticks.
3. In a shallow dish, combine breadcrumbs, grated Parmesan cheese (if using), garlic powder, dried oregano, salt, and pepper.
4. Dip each zucchini stick into the breadcrumb mixture, pressing gently to coat all sides.
5. Place the coated zucchini sticks on the prepared baking sheet in a single layer.
6. Lightly spray the zucchini fries with cooking spray.
7. Bake in the preheated oven for 20-25 minutes, or until the zucchini fries are golden brown and crispy.
8. Remove from the oven and let cool slightly before serving.
9. Serve baked zucchini fries with marinara sauce for dipping.
10. Enjoy these crunchy and flavorful zucchini fries as a healthier alternative to traditional fries!

Nutritional Info (per serving, without Parmesan cheese): Calories: 80 Fat: 2g Carbs: 14g Protein: 3g

Roasted Cauliflower with Tahini Sauce

Prep: 10 mins | Cook: 25 mins | Serves: 4

Ingredients:

- 1 head cauliflower, cut into florets
- 2 tbsp olive oil
- 1 tsp ground cumin
- 1/2 tsp smoked paprika

- Salt and pepper to taste
- Tahini sauce for drizzling
- Fresh parsley, chopped (for garnish)

Ingredients for Tahini Sauce:

- 1/4 cup tahini
- 2 tbsp lemon juice
- 1 clove garlic, minced
- Water (as needed to thin out the sauce)
- Salt to taste

Instructions:

1. Preheat the oven to 425°F (220°C) and line a baking sheet with parchment paper.
2. In a large bowl, toss cauliflower florets with olive oil, ground cumin, smoked paprika, salt, and pepper until evenly coated.
3. Spread the seasoned cauliflower florets out on the prepared baking sheet in a single layer.
4. Roast in the preheated oven for 20-25 minutes, or until cauliflower is tender and caramelized, stirring halfway through.
5. While the cauliflower is roasting, prepare the tahini sauce. In a small bowl, whisk together tahini, lemon juice, minced garlic, and salt. Gradually add water, a tablespoon at a time, until desired consistency is reached.
6. Remove roasted cauliflower from the oven and transfer to a serving dish.
7. Drizzle tahini sauce over the roasted cauliflower.
8. Garnish with fresh chopped parsley before serving.
9. Enjoy this delicious and nutritious roasted cauliflower with creamy tahini sauce as a flavorful side dish or appetizer!

Nutritional Info (per serving, cauliflower only): Calories: 80 Fat: 5g Carbs: 8g Protein: 3g

Nutritional Info (per serving, tahini sauce only): Calories: 70 Fat: 6g Carbs: 3g Protein: 2g

Grilled Pineapple with Coconut Yogurt Dip

Prep: 10 mins | Cook: 5 mins | Serves: 4

Ingredients:

- 1 pineapple, peeled, cored, and sliced into rings
- 1 cup coconut yogurt
- 1 tbsp honey or maple syrup (optional)
- 1 tsp vanilla extract

- Shredded coconut for garnish

Instructions:

1. Preheat the grill to medium-high heat.
2. Place pineapple slices on the grill and cook for 2-3 minutes on each side, or until grill marks appear and pineapple is slightly caramelized.
3. While the pineapple is grilling, prepare the coconut yogurt dip. In a small bowl, mix together coconut yogurt, honey or maple syrup (if using), and vanilla extract until well combined.
4. Remove grilled pineapple from the grill and arrange on a serving platter.
5. Sprinkle shredded coconut over the grilled pineapple for garnish.
6. Serve grilled pineapple with coconut yogurt dip on the side.
7. Enjoy this tropical and refreshing treat as a healthy dessert or snack!

Nutritional Info (per serving, pineapple only): Calories: 80 Fat: 0g Carbs: 20g Protein: 1g

Nutritional Info (per serving, coconut yogurt dip only): Calories: 60 Fat: 3g Carbs: 7g Protein: 2g

SMOOTHIES AND JUICES

Green Smoothie with Spinach, Banana, and Plant-Based Milk

Prep: 5 mins | Cook: 0 mins | Serves: 2

Ingredients:

- 2 cups fresh spinach leaves
- 1 ripe banana
- 1 cup plant-based milk (such as almond, soy, or coconut)
- 1 tbsp chia seeds (optional)
- Honey or maple syrup (optional, for sweetness)

Instructions:

1. In a blender, combine fresh spinach leaves, ripe banana, plant-based milk, and chia seeds (if using).
2. Blend until smooth and creamy.
3. Taste and add honey or maple syrup for sweetness, if desired.
4. Pour into glasses and serve immediately.
5. Enjoy this nutritious and refreshing green smoothie!

Nutritional Info (per serving): Calories: 120 Fat: 3g Carbs: 20g Protein: 5g

Berry and Nut Smoothie with Chia Seeds

Prep: 5 mins | Cook: 0 mins | Serves: 2

Ingredients:

- 1 cup mixed berries (such as strawberries, blueberries, and raspberries)
- 1 ripe banana
- 1 cup plant-based milk (such as almond, soy, or coconut)
- 1/4 cup mixed nuts (such as almonds, walnuts, and cashews)
- 1 tbsp chia seeds

Instructions:

1. In a blender, combine mixed berries, ripe banana, plant-based milk, mixed nuts, and chia seeds.
2. Blend until smooth and creamy.
3. Pour into glasses and serve immediately.
4. Enjoy this antioxidant-rich and satisfying berry and nut smoothie!

Nutritional Info (per serving): Calories: 180 Fat: 9g Carbs: 25g Protein: 6g

Tropical Smoothie with Mango, Pineapple, and Coconut Milk

Prep: 5 mins | Cook: 0 mins | Serves: 2

Ingredients:

- 1 cup chopped mango
- 1 cup chopped pineapple
- 1 ripe banana
- 1 cup coconut milk (canned or carton)
- Ice cubes (optional)

Instructions:

1. In a blender, combine chopped mango, chopped pineapple, ripe banana, and coconut milk.
2. Add ice cubes if desired for a colder smoothie.
3. Blend until smooth and creamy.
4. Pour into glasses and serve immediately.
5. Enjoy this tropical delight of a smoothie!

Nutritional Info (per serving): Calories: 220 Fat: 5g Carbs: 40g Protein: 3g

Vegetable and Fruit Juice with Ginger and Turmeric

Prep: 10 mins | Cook: 0 mins | Serves: 2

Ingredients:

- 2 carrots
- 1 apple
- 1-inch piece of ginger
- 1-inch piece of turmeric (or 1/2 tsp ground turmeric)
- 1 lemon, peeled
- 1 cup water or coconut water
- Ice cubes (optional)

Instructions:

1. Wash and chop carrots, apple, ginger, and turmeric into smaller pieces.
2. In a juicer or blender, combine chopped carrots, apple, ginger, turmeric, peeled lemon, and water or coconut water.
3. Blend or juice until smooth.
4. Strain the juice through a fine mesh sieve if desired for a smoother texture.

5. Serve immediately over ice cubes if desired.
   6. Enjoy this immune-boosting and refreshing vegetable and fruit juice!

Nutritional Info (per serving): Calories: 100 Fat: 0g Carbs: 25g Protein: 1g

Chocolate and Avocado Smoothie with Plant-Based Milk

Prep: 5 mins | Cook: 0 mins | Serves: 2

Ingredients:

- 1 ripe avocado
- 2 tbsp cocoa powder
- 2 cups plant-based milk (such as almond, soy, or oat)
- 2 tbsp honey or maple syrup (optional, for sweetness)
- Ice cubes (optional)

Instructions:

1. Scoop out the flesh of the ripe avocado and place it in a blender.
2. Add cocoa powder, plant-based milk, and honey or maple syrup (if using) to the blender.
3. Blend until smooth and creamy.
4. If desired, add ice cubes for a colder smoothie and blend again until smooth.
5. Pour into glasses and serve immediately.
6. Enjoy this decadent and creamy chocolate avocado smoothie!

Nutritional Info (per serving): Calories: 250 Fat: 14g Carbs: 28g Protein: 5g

Carrot and Orange Juice with Ginger

Prep: 10 mins | Cook: 0 mins | Serves: 2

Ingredients:

- 4 carrots
- 2 oranges, peeled
- 1-inch piece of ginger
- Ice cubes (optional)

Instructions:

1. Wash and peel carrots. Chop them into smaller pieces.
2. Peel oranges and remove any seeds.
3. Peel ginger and cut it into smaller pieces.
4. In a juicer or blender, combine chopped carrots, peeled oranges, and ginger.
5. Blend or juice until smooth.

6. Strain the juice through a fine mesh sieve if desired for a smoother texture.
7. Serve immediately over ice cubes if desired.
8. Enjoy this refreshing and vitamin-packed carrot and orange juice!

Nutritional Info (per serving): Calories: 120 Fat: 0g Carbs: 28g Protein: 2g

Peanut Butter and Banana Smoothie with Oats

Prep: 5 mins | Cook: 0 mins | Serves: 2

Ingredients:

- 2 ripe bananas
- 2 tbsp peanut butter
- 2 tbsp rolled oats
- 2 cups plant-based milk (such as almond, soy, or coconut)
- Ice cubes (optional)

Instructions:

1. Peel ripe bananas and place them in a blender.
2. Add peanut butter, rolled oats, and plant-based milk to the blender.
3. Blend until smooth and creamy.
4. If desired, add ice cubes for a colder smoothie and blend again until smooth.
5. Pour into glasses and serve immediately.
6. Enjoy this nutritious and filling peanut butter and banana smoothie!

Nutritional Info (per serving): Calories: 300 Fat: 12g Carbs: 40g Protein: 9g

Blueberry and Kale Smoothie with Almond Milk

Prep: 5 mins | Cook: 0 mins | Serves: 2

Ingredients:

- 1 cup fresh or frozen blueberries
- 1 cup kale leaves, stems removed
- 1 ripe banana
- 1 cup almond milk
- 1 tbsp honey or maple syrup (optional, for sweetness)
- Ice cubes (optional)

Instructions:

1. In a blender, combine blueberries, kale leaves, ripe banana, almond milk, and honey or maple syrup (if using).
2. Blend until smooth and creamy.

3. If desired, add ice cubes for a colder smoothie and blend again until smooth.
4. Pour into glasses and serve immediately.
5. Enjoy this antioxidant-rich and nutritious blueberry and kale smoothie!

Nutritional Info (per serving): Calories: 150 Fat: 3g Carbs: 30g Protein: 3g

Mango and Spinach Smoothie with Plant-Based Yogurt

Prep: 5 mins | Cook: 0 mins | Serves: 2

Ingredients:

- 1 cup chopped mango
- 1 cup fresh spinach leaves
- 1 ripe banana
- 1/2 cup plant-based yogurt (such as coconut or almond)
- 1/2 cup water or coconut water
- Ice cubes (optional)

Instructions:

1. In a blender, combine chopped mango, fresh spinach leaves, ripe banana, plant-based yogurt, and water or coconut water.
2. Blend until smooth and creamy.
3. If desired, add ice cubes for a colder smoothie and blend again until smooth.
4. Pour into glasses and serve immediately.
5. Enjoy this tropical and refreshing mango and spinach smoothie!

Nutritional Info (per serving): Calories: 200 Fat: 2g Carbs: 40g Protein: 5g

Strawberry and Beet Smoothie with Coconut Water

Prep: 5 mins | Cook: 0 mins | Serves: 2

Ingredients:

- 1 cup chopped strawberries
- 1 small beet, peeled and chopped
- 1 ripe banana
- 1/2 cup coconut water
- 1 tbsp honey or maple syrup (optional, for sweetness)
- Ice cubes (optional)

Instructions:

1. In a blender, combine chopped strawberries, chopped beet, ripe banana, coconut water, and honey or maple syrup (if using).

2. Blend until smooth and creamy.
3. If desired, add ice cubes for a colder smoothie and blend again until smooth.
4. Pour into glasses and serve immediately.
5. Enjoy this vibrant and nutrient-packed strawberry and beet smoothie!

Nutritional Info (per serving): Calories: 180 Fat: 1g Carbs: 40g Protein: 3g

Pineapple and Mint Smoothie with Plant-Based Milk

Prep: 5 mins | Cook: 0 mins | Serves: 2

Ingredients:

- 1 cup chopped pineapple
- 1/4 cup fresh mint leaves
- 1 ripe banana
- 1 cup plant-based milk (such as almond, soy, or oat)
- 1 tbsp honey or maple syrup (optional, for sweetness)
- Ice cubes (optional)

Instructions:

1. In a blender, combine chopped pineapple, fresh mint leaves, ripe banana, plant-based milk, and honey or maple syrup (if using).
2. Blend until smooth and creamy.
3. If desired, add ice cubes for a colder smoothie and blend again until smooth.
4. Pour into glasses and serve immediately.
5. Enjoy this refreshing and tropical pineapple and mint smoothie!

Nutritional Info (per serving): Calories: 180 Fat: 3g Carbs: 40g Protein: 3g

Green Juice with Cucumber, Celery, and Apple

Prep: 10 mins | Cook: 0 mins | Serves: 2

Ingredients:

- 1 cucumber
- 2 celery stalks
- 1 green apple
- 1-inch piece of ginger
- 1 lemon, peeled
- 1 cup water or coconut water
- Ice cubes (optional)

Instructions:

1. Wash and chop cucumber, celery stalks, green apple, and ginger into smaller pieces.
2. Peel lemon and remove any seeds.
3. In a juicer or blender, combine chopped cucumber, celery stalks, green apple, ginger, peeled lemon, and water or coconut water.
4. Blend or juice until smooth.
5. Strain the juice through a fine mesh sieve if desired for a smoother texture.
6. Serve immediately over ice cubes if desired.
7. Enjoy this refreshing and detoxifying green juice!

Nutritional Info (per serving): Calories: 70 Fat: 0g Carbs: 18g Protein: 1g

Chocolate and Peanut Butter Smoothie with Plant-Based Protein Powder

Prep: 5 mins | Cook: 0 mins | Serves: 2

Ingredients:

- 2 tbsp cocoa powder
- 2 tbsp peanut butter
- 1 scoop plant-based protein powder (chocolate flavored)
- 2 cups plant-based milk (such as almond, soy, or oat)
- 1 ripe banana
- Ice cubes (optional)

Instructions:

1. In a blender, combine cocoa powder, peanut butter, plant-based protein powder, plant-based milk, and ripe banana.
2. Blend until smooth and creamy.
3. If desired, add ice cubes for a colder smoothie and blend again until smooth.
4. Pour into glasses and serve immediately.
5. Enjoy this indulgent and protein-packed chocolate and peanut butter smoothie!

Nutritional Info (per serving): Calories: 320 Fat: 10g Carbs: 40g Protein: 20g

Tropical Green Smoothie with Spinach, Mango, and Coconut Milk

Prep: 5 mins | Cook: 0 mins | Serves: 2

Ingredients:

- 2 cups fresh spinach leaves
- 1 cup chopped mango
- 1 ripe banana
- 1 cup coconut milk
- 1 tbsp honey or maple syrup (optional, for sweetness)
- Ice cubes (optional)

Instructions:

1. In a blender, combine fresh spinach leaves, chopped mango, ripe banana, coconut milk, and honey or maple syrup (if using).
2. Blend until smooth and creamy.
3. If desired, add ice cubes for a colder smoothie and blend again until smooth.
4. Pour into glasses and serve immediately.
5. Enjoy this tropical and nutritious green smoothie!

Nutritional Info (per serving): Calories: 200 Fat: 7g Carbs: 35g Protein: 3g

Watermelon and Lime Juice with Mint

Prep: 10 mins | Cook: 0 mins | Serves: 2

Ingredients:

- 2 cups chopped watermelon
- Juice of 2 limes
- 1/4 cup fresh mint leaves
- 1 cup water or coconut water
- Ice cubes (optional)

Instructions:

1. In a blender, combine chopped watermelon, lime juice, fresh mint leaves, and water or coconut water.
2. Blend until smooth.
3. Strain the juice through a fine mesh sieve if desired for a smoother texture.
4. Serve immediately over ice cubes if desired.
5. Enjoy this refreshing and hydrating watermelon lime juice!

Nutritional Info (per serving): Calories: 80 Fat: 0g Carbs: 20g Protein: 1g

BAKED GOODS AND DESSERTS

Vegan Banana Bread with Walnuts

Prep: 15 mins | Cook: 50 mins | Serves: 1 loaf

Ingredients:

- 3 ripe bananas, mashed
- 1/3 cup melted coconut oil
- 1/2 cup maple syrup or agave nectar
- 1/4 cup plant-based milk (such as almond or soy)
- 1 tsp vanilla extract
- 1 3/4 cups all-purpose flour (US) / 225g plain flour (UK)
- 1 tsp baking soda
- 1/2 tsp ground cinnamon
- 1/4 tsp salt
- 1/2 cup chopped walnuts

Instructions:

1. Preheat your oven to 350°F (175°C). Grease a 9x5-inch loaf pan and set aside.
2. In a large mixing bowl, mash the ripe bananas until smooth.
3. Add melted coconut oil, maple syrup or agave nectar, plant-based milk, and vanilla extract to the mashed bananas. Stir until well combined.
4. In a separate bowl, whisk together the all-purpose flour, baking soda, ground cinnamon, and salt.
5. Gradually add the dry ingredients to the wet ingredients, stirring until just combined. Be careful not to overmix.
6. Gently fold in the chopped walnuts.
7. Pour the batter into the prepared loaf pan and spread it evenly.
8. Bake in the preheated oven for 50-60 minutes, or until a toothpick inserted into the center comes out clean.
9. Remove from the oven and allow the banana bread to cool in the pan for 10 minutes before transferring it to a wire rack to cool completely.
10. Once cooled, slice and serve. Enjoy this moist and delicious vegan banana bread!

Nutritional Info (per serving): Calories: 220 Fat: 9g Carbs: 32g Protein: 3g

Oatmeal and Apple Baked Crisp with Cinnamon

Prep: 15 mins | Cook: 35 mins | Serves: 6

Ingredients:

- 4 cups peeled and sliced apples (about 4 medium apples)
- 1 tbsp lemon juice
- 1/4 cup maple syrup or agave nectar
- 1/2 tsp ground cinnamon
- 1 cup rolled oats
- 1/4 cup all-purpose flour (US) / 30g plain flour (UK)
- 1/4 cup brown sugar
- 1/4 cup melted coconut oil
- Pinch of salt

Instructions:

1. 1 Preheat your oven to 350°F (175°C). Grease a 9-inch square baking dish and set aside.
2. In a large mixing bowl, combine the sliced apples, lemon juice, maple syrup or agave nectar, and ground cinnamon. Toss until the apples are evenly coated.
3. In a separate bowl, mix together the rolled oats, all-purpose flour, brown sugar, melted coconut oil, and a pinch of salt until crumbly.
4. Spread the apple mixture evenly in the prepared baking dish.
5. Sprinkle the oat mixture over the top of the apples, covering them completely.
6. Bake in the preheated oven for 30-35 minutes, or until the topping is golden brown and the apples are tender.
7. Remove from the oven and let it cool for a few minutes before serving.
8. Serve warm with a scoop of vegan ice cream or a dollop of coconut whipped cream, if desired.
9. Enjoy this comforting and nutritious oatmeal and apple baked crisp!

Nutritional Info (per serving): Calories: 250 Fat: 8g Carbs: 42g Protein: 3g

Chocolate Avocado Pudding with Coconut Whipped Cream

Prep: 10 mins | Cook: 0 mins | Serves: 4

Ingredients:

- 2 ripe avocados
- 1/4 cup cocoa powder
- 1/4 cup maple syrup or agave nectar
- 1 tsp vanilla extract

- Pinch of salt
- Coconut whipped cream, for serving
- Fresh berries, for garnish (optional)

Instructions:

1. Scoop the flesh of the ripe avocados into a food processor or blender.
2. Add cocoa powder, maple syrup or agave nectar, vanilla extract, and a pinch of salt.
3. Blend until smooth and creamy, scraping down the sides of the bowl as needed.
4. Taste and adjust sweetness if necessary by adding more maple syrup or agave nectar.
5. Transfer the chocolate avocado pudding to serving bowls or glasses.
6. Chill in the refrigerator for at least 30 minutes to allow the pudding to set.
7. Serve topped with coconut whipped cream and fresh berries, if desired.
8. Enjoy this rich and indulgent chocolate avocado pudding!

Nutritional Info (per serving): Calories: 200 Fat: 12g Carbs: 24g Protein: 3g

Fruit and Nut Granola Bars

Prep: 15 mins | Cook: 25 mins | Serves: 12 bars

Ingredients:

- 2 cups rolled oats
- 1/2 cup chopped nuts (such as almonds, walnuts, or pecans)
- 1/4 cup dried fruit (such as raisins, cranberries, or chopped apricots)
- 1/4 cup shredded coconut
- 1/4 cup maple syrup or honey
- 1/4 cup melted coconut oil
- 1 tsp vanilla extract
- Pinch of salt
- 1/4 cup chocolate chips (optional)

Instructions:

1. Preheat your oven to 350°F (175°C). Line an 8x8-inch baking pan with parchment paper, leaving some overhang on the sides for easy removal.
2. In a large mixing bowl, combine rolled oats, chopped nuts, dried fruit, shredded coconut, maple syrup or honey, melted coconut oil, vanilla extract, and a pinch of salt. Stir until well combined.
3. If using chocolate chips, fold them into the mixture.
4. Transfer the mixture to the prepared baking pan and press it down firmly and evenly using the back of a spoon or your hands.

5. Bake in the preheated oven for 20-25 minutes, or until the edges are golden brown.
6. Remove from the oven and let it cool completely in the pan.
7. Once cooled, use the parchment paper overhang to lift the granola slab out of the pan.
8. Cut into bars using a sharp knife.
9. Store the granola bars in an airtight container at room temperature for up to a week, or in the refrigerator for longer shelf life.
10. Enjoy these homemade fruit and nut granola bars as a convenient and nutritious snack!

Nutritional Info (per serving): Calories: 180 Fat: 9g Carbs: 22g Protein: 3g

Baked Apples with Cinnamon and Raisins

Prep: 10 mins | Cook: 25 mins | Serves: 4

Ingredients:

- 4 large apples (such as Granny Smith or Honeycrisp)
- 1/4 cup raisins
- 1/4 cup chopped nuts (such as walnuts or pecans)
- 2 tbsp maple syrup or honey
- 1 tsp ground cinnamon
- Pinch of nutmeg (optional)
- 1/2 cup water

Instructions:

1. Preheat your oven to 375°F (190°C). Core the apples and remove the seeds, creating a well in the center for filling.
2. In a small bowl, mix together the raisins, chopped nuts, maple syrup or honey, ground cinnamon, and pinch of nutmeg if using.
3. Stuff each cored apple with the raisin and nut mixture, pressing it down gently.
4. Place the stuffed apples in a baking dish and pour water into the bottom of the dish.
5. Cover the baking dish with aluminum foil and bake in the preheated oven for 20-25 minutes, or until the apples are tender.
6. Remove the foil and bake for an additional 5 minutes to allow the tops to brown slightly.
7. Remove from the oven and let the baked apples cool slightly before serving.
8. Serve warm, optionally topped with a scoop of vanilla ice cream or a dollop of Greek yogurt.
9. Enjoy these warm and comforting baked apples with cinnamon and raisins!

Nutritional Info (per serving): Calories: 150 Fat: 3g Carbs: 33g Protein: 2g

Vegan Pumpkin Bread with Pecan Streusel

Prep: 15 mins | Cook: 1 hour | Serves: 1 loaf

Ingredients:

For the Bread:

- 1 3/4 cups all-purpose flour (US) / 225g plain flour (UK)
- 1 tsp baking soda
- 1/2 tsp baking powder
- 1/2 tsp salt
- 1 tsp ground cinnamon
- 1/2 tsp ground nutmeg
- 1/4 tsp ground cloves
- 1 cup canned pumpkin puree
- 3/4 cup coconut sugar or brown sugar
- 1/3 cup melted coconut oil
- 1/4 cup plant-based milk (such as almond or soy)
- 1 tsp vanilla extract

For the Pecan Streusel:

- 1/4 cup all-purpose flour (US) / 30g plain flour (UK)
- 1/4 cup chopped pecans
- 2 tbsp coconut sugar or brown sugar
- 2 tbsp melted coconut oil

Instructions:

1. Preheat your oven to 350°F (175°C). Grease a 9x5-inch loaf pan and set aside.
2. In a large mixing bowl, whisk together the all-purpose flour, baking soda, baking powder, salt, ground cinnamon, ground nutmeg, and ground cloves.
3. In a separate bowl, mix together the canned pumpkin puree, coconut sugar or brown sugar, melted coconut oil, plant-based milk, and vanilla extract until well combined.
4. Gradually add the wet ingredients to the dry ingredients, stirring until just combined. Be careful not to overmix.
5. Pour the batter into the prepared loaf pan and spread it evenly.
6. In a small bowl, combine the all-purpose flour, chopped pecans, coconut sugar or brown sugar, and melted coconut oil to make the streusel topping.
7. Sprinkle the streusel evenly over the top of the pumpkin bread batter.
8. Bake in the preheated oven for 55-60 minutes, or until a toothpick inserted into the center comes out clean.

9. Remove from the oven and let the pumpkin bread cool in the pan for 10 minutes before transferring it to a wire rack to cool completely.
10. Once cooled, slice and serve. Enjoy this moist and flavorful vegan pumpkin bread with pecan streusel!

Nutritional Info (per serving): Calories: 220 Fat: 9g Carbs: 32g Protein: 3g

Chocolate and Almond Butter Energy Bites

Prep: 15 mins | Cook: 0 mins | Serves: 12 bites

Ingredients:

- 1 cup rolled oats
- 1/2 cup almond butter
- 1/4 cup maple syrup or honey
- 1/4 cup cocoa powder
- 1 tsp vanilla extract
- Pinch of salt
- 1/4 cup chopped almonds
- 2 tbsp shredded coconut (optional)

Instructions:

1. In a large mixing bowl, combine rolled oats, almond butter, maple syrup or honey, cocoa powder, vanilla extract, and a pinch of salt.
2. Mix until all ingredients are well combined and the mixture is sticky.
3. Fold in chopped almonds and shredded coconut, if using.
4. Using your hands, roll the mixture into small bite-sized balls.
5. Place the energy bites on a baking sheet lined with parchment paper.
6. Refrigerate for at least 30 minutes to allow the bites to firm up.
7. Once firm, transfer the energy bites to an airtight container and store them in the refrigerator.
8. Enjoy these chocolate and almond butter energy bites as a quick and nutritious snack on the go!

Nutritional Info (per serving 1 bite): Calories: 120 Fat: 6g Carbs: 14g Protein: 3g

Lemon and Blueberry Muffins

Prep: 15 mins | Cook: 20 mins | Serves: 12 muffins

Ingredients:

- 2 cups all-purpose flour (US) / 250g plain flour (UK)
- 1/2 cup granulated sugar
- 1 tbsp baking powder
- 1/2 tsp salt
- 1 cup plant-based milk (such as almond or soy)
- 1/3 cup melted coconut oil
- 1/4 cup fresh lemon juice
- Zest of 1 lemon
- 1 tsp vanilla extract
- 1 cup fresh or frozen blueberries

Instructions:

1. Preheat your oven to 375°F (190°C). Line a muffin tin with paper liners or grease the wells with coconut oil.
2. In a large mixing bowl, whisk together the all-purpose flour, granulated sugar, baking powder, and salt.
3. In a separate bowl, mix together the plant-based milk, melted coconut oil, fresh lemon juice, lemon zest, and vanilla extract.
4. Pour the wet ingredients into the dry ingredients and stir until just combined. Be careful not to overmix.
5. Gently fold in the blueberries.
6. Divide the batter evenly among the prepared muffin cups, filling each about 3/4 full.
7. Bake in the preheated oven for 18-20 minutes, or until a toothpick inserted into the center of a muffin comes out clean.
8. Remove from the oven and let the muffins cool in the tin for a few minutes before transferring them to a wire rack to cool completely.
9. Once cooled, serve and enjoy these lemon and blueberry muffins as a delightful treat any time of day!

Nutritional Info (per muffin): Calories: 180 Fat: 6g Carbs: 28g Protein: 3g

Vegan Carrot Cake with Cashew Cream Frosting

Prep: 20 mins | Cook: 30 mins | Serves: 8 slices

Ingredients:

For the Cake:

- 2 cups all-purpose flour (US) / 250g plain flour (UK)
- 1 tsp baking powder
- 1/2 tsp baking soda
- 1/2 tsp salt
- 1 tsp ground cinnamon
- 1/2 tsp ground nutmeg
- 1/2 cup coconut oil, melted
- 1/2 cup maple syrup or agave nectar
- 1/2 cup plant-based milk (such as almond or soy)
- 2 cups grated carrots
- 1/2 cup chopped walnuts (optional)
- 1/2 cup raisins (optional)

For the Cashew Cream Frosting:

- 1 cup raw cashews, soaked in water for at least 4 hours or overnight
- 1/4 cup maple syrup or agave nectar
- 2 tbsp coconut oil, melted
- 2 tbsp lemon juice
- 1 tsp vanilla extract
- Pinch of salt

Instructions:

For the Cake:

1. 1 Preheat your oven to 350°F (175°C). Grease and flour an 8-inch round cake pan or line it with parchment paper.
2. In a large mixing bowl, whisk together the all-purpose flour, baking powder, baking soda, salt, ground cinnamon, and ground nutmeg.
3. In a separate bowl, mix together the melted coconut oil, maple syrup or agave nectar, and plant-based milk until well combined.
4. Gradually add the wet ingredients to the dry ingredients, stirring until just combined.
5. Fold in the grated carrots, chopped walnuts, and raisins, if using.
6. Pour the batter into the prepared cake pan and spread it out evenly.

7. Bake in the preheated oven for 25-30 minutes, or until a toothpick inserted into the center comes out clean.
8. Remove from the oven and let the cake cool in the pan for 10 minutes before transferring it to a wire rack to cool completely.

For the Cashew Cream Frosting:

1. Drain and rinse the soaked cashews. Place them in a high-speed blender or food processor.
2. Add maple syrup or agave nectar, melted coconut oil, lemon juice, vanilla extract, and a pinch of salt.
3. Blend on high until smooth and creamy, scraping down the sides of the blender or food processor as needed.
4. Once the cake has cooled completely, spread the cashew cream frosting evenly over the top.
5. Slice and serve this delicious vegan carrot cake with cashew cream frosting as a delightful dessert!

Nutritional Info (per slice): Calories: 350 Fat: 20g Carbs: 36g Protein: 5g

Baked Pears with Honey and Walnuts

Prep: 10 mins | Cook: 30 mins | Serves: 4

Ingredients:

- 4 ripe but firm pears
- 2 tbsp honey
- 1/4 cup chopped walnuts
- 1 tsp ground cinnamon
- Pinch of nutmeg (optional)
- 2 tbsp melted coconut oil

Instructions:

1. Preheat your oven to 375°F (190°C). Line a baking dish with parchment paper.
2. Cut the pears in half lengthwise and remove the cores with a spoon or melon baller, creating a hollow in each half.
3. Place the pear halves cut side up in the prepared baking dish.
4. In a small bowl, mix together the honey, chopped walnuts, ground cinnamon, and pinch of nutmeg if using.
5. Spoon the honey and walnut mixture evenly into the hollows of the pear halves.
6. Drizzle the melted coconut oil over the top of the pear halves.

7. Bake in the preheated oven for 25-30 minutes, or until the pears are tender and caramelized.
8. Remove from the oven and let the baked pears cool slightly before serving.
9. Serve warm, optionally topped with a dollop of Greek yogurt or a scoop of vanilla ice cream.
10. Enjoy these baked pears with honey and walnuts as a simple and elegant dessert!

Nutritional Info (per serving): Calories: 180 Fat: 8g Carbs: 28g Protein: 2g

Coconut and Dark Chocolate Truffles

Prep: 20 mins | Cook: 0 mins | Chill: 1 hour | Makes: 12 truffles

Ingredients:

- 1/2 cup coconut cream
- 8 oz (225g) dark chocolate, finely chopped
- 1 tsp vanilla extract
- Pinch of salt
- 1/2 cup shredded coconut, for coating
- Cocoa powder, for dusting (optional)

Instructions:

1. 1 In a small saucepan, heat the coconut cream over medium heat until it just begins to simmer.
2. Place the chopped dark chocolate in a heatproof bowl. Pour the hot coconut cream over the chocolate and let it sit for 1-2 minutes.
3. Stir the chocolate and coconut cream together until smooth and well combined. If needed, you can gently heat the mixture in the microwave in 10-second intervals, stirring in between, until fully melted and smooth.
4. Stir in the vanilla extract and a pinch of salt.
5. Cover the bowl with plastic wrap and refrigerate the chocolate mixture for at least 1 hour, or until firm.
6. Once chilled, use a small spoon or melon baller to scoop out portions of the chocolate mixture and roll them into balls with your hands.
7. Roll each truffle in shredded coconut until evenly coated.
8. If desired, dust the truffles with cocoa powder for an extra touch of flavor.
9. Place the coated truffles on a baking sheet lined with parchment paper.
10. Refrigerate the truffles for another 15-20 minutes to set.
11. Once set, transfer the truffles to an airtight container and store them in the refrigerator until ready to serve.

12. Enjoy these decadent coconut and dark chocolate truffles as a delicious treat or homemade gift!

Nutritional Info (per truffle): Calories: 120 Fat: 9g Carbs: 9g Protein: 2g

Oatmeal and Raisin Cookies

Prep: 15 mins | Cook: 12 mins | Makes: 12 cookies

Ingredients:

- 1 cup rolled oats
- 1/2 cup all-purpose flour (US) / 60g plain flour (UK)
- 1/2 tsp baking powder
- 1/2 tsp ground cinnamon
- Pinch of salt
- 1/4 cup coconut oil, melted
- 1/4 cup maple syrup or honey
- 1/2 tsp vanilla extract
- 1/4 cup raisins

Instructions:

1. Preheat your oven to 350°F (175°C). Line a baking sheet with parchment paper.
2. In a large mixing bowl, combine the rolled oats, all-purpose flour, baking powder, ground cinnamon, and a pinch of salt.
3. In a separate bowl, whisk together the melted coconut oil, maple syrup or honey, and vanilla extract.
4. Pour the wet ingredients into the dry ingredients and stir until well combined.
5. Fold in the raisins until evenly distributed throughout the dough.
6. Use a spoon or cookie scoop to portion out the dough and roll it into balls. Place the balls of dough onto the prepared baking sheet, spacing them apart.
7. Use your fingers or the back of a fork to flatten each ball of dough into a cookie shape.
8. Bake in the preheated oven for 10-12 minutes, or until the edges are golden brown.
9. Remove from the oven and let the cookies cool on the baking sheet for 5 minutes before transferring them to a wire rack to cool completely.
10. Once cooled, serve and enjoy these delicious oatmeal and raisin cookies with a glass of plant-based milk or your favorite hot beverage!

Nutritional Info (per cookie): Calories: 120 Fat: 5g Carbs: 18g Protein: 2g

Vegan Brownies with Walnuts

Prep: 15 mins | Cook: 30 mins | Serves: 12 brownies

Ingredients:

- 1 cup all-purpose flour (US) / 120g plain flour (UK)
- 1 cup granulated sugar (US) / 200g caster sugar (UK)
- 1/2 cup cocoa powder (US) / 50g cocoa powder (UK)
- 1 tsp baking powder
- 1/2 tsp salt
- 1/2 cup water
- 1/2 cup vegetable oil
- 1 tsp vanilla extract
- 1/2 cup chopped walnuts

Instructions:

1. Preheat your oven to 350°F (175°C). Grease a 9x9 inch (23x23 cm) baking pan or line it with parchment paper.
2. In a large mixing bowl, combine the flour, sugar, cocoa powder, baking powder, and salt.
3. Add the water, vegetable oil, and vanilla extract to the dry ingredients. Stir until well combined.
4. Fold in the chopped walnuts.
5. Pour the batter into the prepared baking pan and spread it evenly.
6. Bake in the preheated oven for 25-30 minutes, or until a toothpick inserted into the center comes out clean.
7. Allow the brownies to cool in the pan before cutting into squares.
8. Serve and enjoy these rich, chocolatey vegan brownies as a delightful dessert or snack.

Nutritional Info (per brownie): Calories: 200 Fat: 11g Carbs: 26g Protein: 3g

Baked Peaches with Maple and Cinnamon

Prep: 10 mins | Cook: 20 mins | Serves: 4

Ingredients:

- 4 ripe peaches, halved and pitted
- 2 tbsp maple syrup
- 1 tsp ground cinnamon
- 1/4 cup chopped pecans
- 1 tbsp coconut oil, melted

Instructions:

1. Preheat your oven to 350°F (175°C).
2. Place the peach halves in a baking dish, cut side up.
3. Drizzle the maple syrup over the peaches and sprinkle with ground cinnamon.
4. In a small bowl, combine the chopped pecans and melted coconut oil.
5. Spoon the pecan mixture into the center of each peach half.
6. Bake in the preheated oven for 20 minutes, or until the peaches are tender and caramelized.
7. Serve the baked peaches warm, with a dollop of coconut yogurt or plant-based ice cream if desired.
8. Enjoy these delicious and healthy baked peaches as a sweet treat or dessert.

Nutritional Info (per serving): Calories: 120 Fat: 7g Carbs: 15g Protein: 1g

Coconut and Berry Chia Pudding Parfaits

Prep: 10 mins | Chill: 2 hours | Serves: 4

Ingredients:

- 1/2 cup chia seeds
- 2 cups coconut milk
- 2 tbsp maple syrup
- 1 tsp vanilla extract
- 1 cup mixed berries (strawberries, blueberries, raspberries)
- 1/4 cup shredded coconut

Instructions:

1. In a medium bowl, combine the chia seeds, coconut milk, maple syrup, and vanilla extract. Stir well to combine.
2. Cover the bowl and refrigerate for at least 2 hours, or overnight, until the mixture thickens into a pudding-like consistency.
3. Once the chia pudding is set, give it a good stir to break up any clumps.
4. In serving glasses or bowls, layer the chia pudding with mixed berries and shredded coconut.
5. Repeat the layers until all ingredients are used, finishing with a layer of berries and a sprinkle of shredded coconut on top.
6. Serve immediately or keep refrigerated until ready to serve.
7. Enjoy these creamy and refreshing coconut and berry chia pudding parfaits as a nutritious breakfast or snack.

Nutritional Info (per serving): Calories: 180 Fat: 10g Carbs: 21g Protein: 4g

BEVERAGES AND CONDIMENTS

Herbal Teas

Prep: 5 mins | Cook: 5 mins | Serves: 4 cups

Ingredients:

- 4 cups water (US) / 1 liter water (UK)
- 4 herbal tea bags (chamomile, peppermint, or ginger)
- Honey or lemon, to taste (optional)

Instructions:

1. Bring water to a boil in a kettle or saucepan.
2. Pour the hot water over the tea bags in a teapot or heatproof jug.
3. Let the tea steep for 5 minutes, or longer for a stronger flavor.
4. Remove the tea bags and sweeten with honey or add a slice of lemon if desired.
5. Serve hot or let cool and serve over ice for a refreshing iced tea.

Nutritional Info (per cup): Calories: 0 Fat: 0g Carbs: 0g Protein: 0g

Nut and Plant-Based Milk (Almond Milk)

Prep: 10 mins | Soak: 8 hours | Serves: 4 cups

Ingredients:

- 1 cup raw almonds (US) / 150g raw almonds (UK)
- 4 cups water (US) / 1 liter water (UK)
- 1-2 dates, pitted (optional, for sweetness)
- 1 tsp vanilla extract (optional)

Instructions:

1. Soak the almonds in water overnight or for at least 8 hours.
2. Drain and rinse the almonds.
3. In a blender, combine the soaked almonds, fresh water, dates, and vanilla extract.
4. Blend on high until smooth and creamy.
5. Strain the mixture through a nut milk bag or fine mesh strainer into a jug.
6. Store the almond milk in the refrigerator for up to 4 days. Shake well before each use.

Nutritional Info (per cup): Calories: 40 Fat: 3g Carbs: 2g Protein: 1g

Fresh Fruit-Infused Water

Prep: 5 mins | Infuse: 1 hour | Serves: 8 cups

Ingredients:

- 8 cups water (US) / 2 liters water (UK)
- 1 lemon, sliced
- 1 cucumber, sliced
- A handful of fresh mint leaves
- 1 cup fresh berries (strawberries, blueberries, or raspberries)

Instructions:

1. Add all the ingredients to a large pitcher.
2. Stir well and let sit in the refrigerator for at least 1 hour to allow the flavors to infuse.
3. Serve chilled, adding ice if desired.

Nutritional Info (per cup): Calories: 0 Fat: 0g Carbs: 0g Protein: 0g

Homemade Nut Butter (Peanut Butter)

Prep: 10 mins | Cook: 10 mins | Serves: 2 cups

Ingredients:

- 2 cups roasted peanuts (US) / 300g roasted peanuts (UK)
- 1-2 tbsp honey (optional)
- 1/2 tsp salt (optional)

Instructions:

1. Place the roasted peanuts in a food processor.
2. Process on high until smooth and creamy, scraping down the sides as needed.
3. Add honey and salt, if using, and process again until well mixed.
4. Transfer the peanut butter to a jar and store in the refrigerator for up to 3 weeks.

Nutritional Info (per tbsp): Calories: 90 Fat: 8g Carbs: 3g Protein: 4g

Vegetable and Herb Pesto

Prep: 10 mins | Serves: 1 cup

Ingredients:

- 2 cups fresh basil leaves (US) / 50g fresh basil leaves (UK)
- 1/4 cup pine nuts (US) / 30g pine nuts (UK)
- 2 cloves garlic
- 1/2 cup olive oil (US) / 120ml olive oil (UK)

- 1/4 cup nutritional yeast (optional)
- Salt and pepper to taste

Instructions:

1. In a food processor, combine the basil, pine nuts, and garlic. Pulse until finely chopped.
2. With the processor running, slowly add the olive oil until the mixture is smooth and emulsified.
3. Add the nutritional yeast (if using) and season with salt and pepper to taste.
4. Store in an airtight container in the refrigerator for up to 1 week.

Nutritional Info (per tbsp): Calories: 90 Fat: 9g Carbs: 1g Protein: 1g

Roasted Chickpeas with Spices

Prep: 10 mins | Cook: 30 mins | Serves: 4

Ingredients:

- 2 cans (15 oz each) chickpeas, drained and rinsed (US) / 2 cans (400g each) chickpeas, drained and rinsed (UK)
- 2 tbsp olive oil (US) / 30 ml olive oil (UK)
- 1 tsp paprika
- 1 tsp ground cumin
- 1/2 tsp garlic powder
- Salt and pepper to taste

Instructions:

1. Preheat your oven to 400°F (200°C).
2. Spread the chickpeas on a baking sheet and pat them dry with a paper towel.
3. In a large bowl, toss the chickpeas with olive oil, paprika, cumin, garlic powder, salt, and pepper until evenly coated.
4. Spread the seasoned chickpeas in a single layer on the baking sheet.
5. Roast in the preheated oven for 25-30 minutes, shaking the pan halfway through, until crispy and golden brown.
6. Let cool slightly before serving.

Nutritional Info (per serving): Calories: 180 Fat: 7g Carbs: 23g Protein: 6g

Baked Sweet Potato Fries with Avocado Dipping Sauce

Prep: 15 mins | Cook: 30 mins | Serves: 4

Ingredients:

- 2 large sweet potatoes (US) / 2 large sweet potatoes (UK)
- 2 tbsp olive oil (US) / 30 ml olive oil (UK)
- 1 tsp paprika
- 1/2 tsp garlic powder
- Salt and pepper to taste
- 1 ripe avocado
- 1/2 cup plain Greek yogurt (US) / 120g plain Greek yogurt (UK)
- 1 tbsp lime juice (US) / 15 ml lime juice (UK)
- 1 clove garlic, minced
- Salt to taste

Instructions:

1. Preheat your oven to 425°F (220°C).
2. Peel and cut the sweet potatoes into thin fries.
3. Toss the sweet potato fries in a bowl with olive oil, paprika, garlic powder, salt, and pepper.
4. Spread the fries on a baking sheet in a single layer.
5. Bake for 25-30 minutes, flipping halfway through, until crispy and golden brown.
6. While the fries bake, make the avocado dipping sauce by blending the avocado, Greek yogurt, lime juice, minced garlic, and salt in a food processor until smooth.
7. Serve the sweet potato fries warm with the avocado dipping sauce.

Nutritional Info (per serving): Calories: 250 Fat: 10g Carbs: 37g Protein: 4g

Kale Chips with Nutritional Yeast

Prep: 10 mins | Cook: 15 mins | Serves: 4

Ingredients:

- 1 large bunch kale (US) / 1 large bunch kale (UK)
- 1 tbsp olive oil (US) / 15 ml olive oil (UK)
- 2 tbsp nutritional yeast (US) / 15g nutritional yeast (UK)
- Salt and pepper to taste

Instructions:

1. Preheat your oven to 350°F (175°C).

2. Wash and thoroughly dry the kale, then remove the leaves from the thick stems and tear into bite-sized pieces.
3. Toss the kale with olive oil in a large bowl, then sprinkle with nutritional yeast, salt, and pepper.
4. Spread the kale in a single layer on a baking sheet.
5. Bake for 10-15 minutes, until the edges are brown but not burnt.
6. Let cool before serving.

Nutritional Info (per serving): Calories: 80 Fat: 5g Carbs: 7g Protein: 3g

Hummus and Veggie Wraps with Whole Grain Tortillas

Prep: 15 mins | Cook: 0 mins | Serves: 4

Ingredients:

- 4 whole grain tortillas (US) / 4 whole grain tortillas (UK)
- 1 cup hummus (US) / 240g hummus (UK)
- 1 cucumber, sliced
- 1 bell pepper, sliced
- 1 carrot, grated
- 1 cup baby spinach leaves (US) / 30g baby spinach leaves (UK)
- Salt and pepper to taste

Instructions:

1. Spread 1/4 cup hummus on each tortilla.
2. Layer the cucumber, bell pepper, carrot, and spinach evenly over the hummus.
3. Season with salt and pepper to taste.
4. Roll up the tortillas tightly and slice in half if desired.
5. Serve immediately or wrap in foil for a convenient on-the-go snack.

Nutritional Info (per serving): Calories: 220 Fat: 8g Carbs: 30g Protein: 7g

Roasted Beet and Orange Salad with Walnuts

Prep: 10 mins | Cook: 40 mins | Serves: 4

Ingredients:

- 4 medium beets (US) / 4 medium beets (UK)
- 2 oranges, segmented
- 1/2 cup walnuts, toasted (US) / 50g walnuts, toasted (UK)
- 4 cups mixed greens (US) / 100g mixed greens (UK)
- 1/4 cup olive oil (US) / 60 ml olive oil (UK)

- 2 tbsp balsamic vinegar (US) / 30 ml balsamic vinegar (UK)
- Salt and pepper to taste

Instructions:

1. Preheat your oven to 400°F (200°C).
2. Wrap each beet in aluminum foil and place them on a baking sheet. Roast for 40 minutes or until tender.
3. Let the beets cool, then peel and slice them.
4. In a large bowl, combine the roasted beets, orange segments, toasted walnuts, and mixed greens.
5. In a small bowl, whisk together the olive oil, balsamic vinegar, salt, and pepper.
6. Drizzle the dressing over the salad and toss to combine.
7. Serve immediately.

Nutritional Info (per serving): Calories: 250 Fat: 18g Carbs: 21g Protein: 4g

Quinoa and Black Bean Stuffed Avocados

Prep: 15 mins | Cook: 15 mins | Serves: 4

Ingredients:

- 1 cup quinoa, cooked (US) / 170g quinoa, cooked (UK)
- 1 can (15 oz) black beans, drained and rinsed (US) / 1 can (400g) black beans, drained and rinsed (UK)
- 2 tbsp lime juice (US) / 30 ml lime juice (UK)
- 1/4 cup chopped cilantro (US) / 15g chopped cilantro (UK)
- 1/2 cup cherry tomatoes, halved (US) / 75g cherry tomatoes, halved (UK)
- 4 large avocados, halved and pitted
- Salt and pepper to taste

Instructions:

1. In a medium bowl, mix the cooked quinoa, black beans, lime juice, chopped cilantro, and cherry tomatoes.
2. Season with salt and pepper to taste.
3. Scoop the quinoa mixture into the avocado halves.
4. Serve immediately.

Nutritional Info (per serving): Calories: 350 Fat: 25g Carbs: 30g Protein: 7g

Baked Zucchini Fries with Marinara Sauce

Prep: 15 mins | Cook: 25 mins | Serves: 4

Ingredients:

- 3 medium zucchinis (US) / 3 medium courgettes (UK)
- 1 cup breadcrumbs (US) / 100g breadcrumbs (UK)
- 1/4 cup grated Parmesan cheese (US) / 25g grated Parmesan cheese (UK)
- 2 large eggs (US) / 2 large eggs (UK)
- 1 tsp garlic powder
- Salt and pepper to taste
- 1 cup marinara sauce, for dipping (US) / 240g marinara sauce, for dipping (UK)

Instructions:

1. Preheat your oven to 425°F (220°C). Line a baking sheet with parchment paper.
2. Cut the zucchinis into sticks.
3. In a shallow dish, mix the breadcrumbs, grated Parmesan, garlic powder, salt, and pepper.
4. In another shallow dish, beat the eggs.
5. Dip each zucchini stick into the beaten eggs, then coat with the breadcrumb mixture.
6. Arrange the zucchini fries on the baking sheet in a single layer.
7. Bake for 20-25 minutes, until golden and crispy.
8. Serve with warm marinara sauce for dipping.

Nutritional Info (per serving): Calories: 210 Fat: 9g Carbs: 25g Protein: 8g

Roasted Cauliflower with Tahini Sauce

Prep: 10 mins | Cook: 30 mins | Serves: 4

Ingredients:

- 1 large cauliflower head, cut into florets (US) / 1 large cauliflower head, cut into florets (UK)
- 2 tbsp olive oil (US) / 30 ml olive oil (UK)
- 1/2 tsp ground cumin
- Salt and pepper to taste
- 1/4 cup tahini (US) / 60g tahini (UK)
- 2 tbsp lemon juice (US) / 30 ml lemon juice (UK)
- 1 clove garlic, minced
- 2-3 tbsp water (US) / 30-45 ml water (UK)

Instructions:

1. Preheat your oven to 425°F (220°C).
2. Toss the cauliflower florets with olive oil, ground cumin, salt, and pepper.
3. Spread the cauliflower on a baking sheet in a single layer.
4. Roast for 25-30 minutes, until tender and golden brown.
5. Meanwhile, prepare the tahini sauce by whisking together the tahini, lemon juice, minced garlic, and water until smooth.
6. Drizzle the tahini sauce over the roasted cauliflower before serving.

Nutritional Info (per serving): Calories: 180 Fat: 14g Carbs: 12g Protein: 4g

Tofu Stir-Fry with Broccoli and Cashews

Prep: 15 mins | Cook: 20 mins | Serves: 4

Ingredients:

- 1 block (14 oz) firm tofu, cubed (US) / 400g firm tofu, cubed (UK)
- 2 cups broccoli florets (US) / 200g broccoli florets (UK)
- 1 red bell pepper, sliced (US) / 1 red pepper, sliced (UK)
- 1 cup snap peas (US) / 100g snap peas (UK)
- 1/2 cup cashews (US) / 50g cashews (UK)
- 3 tbsp soy sauce (US) / 45 ml soy sauce (UK)
- 2 tbsp sesame oil (US) / 30 ml sesame oil (UK)
- 1 tbsp grated ginger (US) / 15g grated ginger (UK)
- 2 cloves garlic, minced
- 1 tbsp cornstarch (US) / 1 tbsp cornflour (UK) mixed with 2 tbsp water (US) / 30 ml water (UK)
- Cooked brown rice, for serving

Instructions:

1. Heat 1 tbsp sesame oil in a large skillet or wok over medium-high heat.
2. Add the cubed tofu and cook until golden brown, about 5-7 minutes. Remove and set aside.
3. In the same skillet, heat the remaining sesame oil. Add the ginger and garlic, and sauté for 1 minute.
4. Add the broccoli, red bell pepper, and snap peas. Stir-fry for 5-7 minutes until tender-crisp.
5. Return the tofu to the skillet, add the soy sauce, and toss to coat.
6. Stir in the cashews and the cornstarch mixture, and cook until the sauce has thickened, about 2-3 minutes.

7. Serve over cooked brown rice.

Nutritional Info (per serving): Calories: 350 Fat: 20g Carbs: 25g Protein: 15g

Lentil and Vegetable Meatballs with Marinara Sauce

Prep: 20 mins | Cook: 30 mins | Serves: 4

Ingredients:

- 1 cup cooked lentils (US) / 200g cooked lentils (UK)
- 1/2 cup breadcrumbs (US) / 50g breadcrumbs (UK)
- 1/4 cup grated carrot (US) / 30g grated carrot (UK)
- 1/4 cup chopped onion (US) / 30g chopped onion (UK)
- 2 cloves garlic, minced
- 1 tbsp tomato paste (US) / 15g tomato paste (UK)
- 1 tsp dried oregano
- 1 tsp dried basil
- Salt and pepper to taste
- 2 cups marinara sauce (US) / 500g marinara sauce (UK)
- Cooked spaghetti, for serving

Instructions:

1. Preheat your oven to 375°F (190°C) and line a baking sheet with parchment paper.
2. In a large bowl, combine the cooked lentils, breadcrumbs, grated carrot, chopped onion, garlic, tomato paste, oregano, basil, salt, and pepper.
3. Form the mixture into small meatballs and place them on the prepared baking sheet.
4. Bake for 20-25 minutes until firm and lightly browned.
5. In a saucepan, heat the marinara sauce over medium heat.
6. Add the baked lentil meatballs to the sauce and simmer for 5-10 minutes.
7. Serve the meatballs and sauce over cooked spaghetti.

Nutritional Info (per serving): Calories: 300 Fat: 6g Carbs: 45g Protein: 12g

CONCLUSION

Creating a cookbook tailored for those managing hemochromatosis involves more than just providing recipes; it is about offering a resource that can enhance quality of life through mindful eating. Hemochromatosis, characterized by excess iron absorption, demands a dietary approach that carefully balances nutritional needs while minimizing iron intake. This cookbook has been crafted with the specific goal of helping individuals manage their iron levels without compromising on taste or variety.

Throughout this cookbook, the recipes have been designed with low-iron ingredients, focusing on plant-based options, which are naturally lower in iron compared to animal-based foods. Emphasizing plant-based proteins such as legumes, tofu, and quinoa not only supports a low-iron diet but also contributes to overall health through increased fiber intake and reduced saturated fat consumption. The inclusion of vibrant vegetables and fruits ensures that each meal is packed with essential vitamins and antioxidants, promoting overall wellness.

One of the key strategies highlighted in this cookbook is the use of ingredients that inhibit iron absorption. Foods high in calcium, such as fortified plant-based milks and certain leafy greens, can reduce iron absorption when consumed with high-iron foods. Additionally, polyphenols found in tea, coffee, and some plant-based foods also play a role in inhibiting iron absorption. By incorporating these inhibitors into the recipes, this cookbook helps manage iron intake effectively.

Convenience and simplicity have been considered in every recipe. Living with a chronic condition can be demanding, and the last thing anyone needs is to spend excessive time and energy on meal preparation. These recipes are designed to be straightforward, with easy-to-follow steps, and many can be prepared in advance. This approach not only saves time but also ensures that you always have a nutritious meal on hand, reducing the temptation to resort to iron-rich convenience foods.

This cookbook also emphasizes the importance of flavor and satisfaction. Managing hemochromatosis should not mean sacrificing the joy of eating. The recipes include a variety of herbs, spices, and flavor combinations to ensure that meals are not only healthy but also delicious. From the savory richness of a lentil and vegetable curry to the sweet satisfaction of a vegan carrot cake with cashew cream frosting, each recipe aims to delight the palate.

Moreover, this cookbook encourages a holistic approach to health. While diet is crucial in managing hemochromatosis, other lifestyle factors such as regular exercise, adequate hydration, and stress management are also important. A balanced lifestyle supports overall health and can enhance the effectiveness of a low-iron diet.

In addition to recipes, this cookbook provides valuable tips and guidance on meal planning and preparation. Understanding which foods to include and which to avoid, as well as how to combine them for optimal nutrition and minimal iron absorption, empowers individuals to take control of their health. By offering practical advice on grocery shopping, ingredient substitutions, and cooking techniques, this cookbook serves as a comprehensive guide for those living with hemochromatosis.

Ultimately, the goal of this cookbook is to make managing hemochromatosis more manageable and less daunting. It aims to provide a sense of normalcy and enjoyment in daily meals while supporting health and well-being. The recipes and tips within these pages are designed to help you live a vibrant, healthy life, enjoying delicious food without the worry of excessive iron intake.

Living with hemochromatosis requires diligence and care, but with the right tools and resources, it is entirely possible to lead a fulfilling and healthy life. This cookbook is a step towards that goal, offering a collection of delicious, low-iron recipes that are easy to prepare and enjoyable to eat. By embracing a mindful approach to eating and utilizing the recipes and tips provided, you can effectively manage your iron levels and enjoy a varied and satisfying diet.

Thank you for choosing this cookbook as a part of your health journey. May it inspire you to explore new flavors, create nourishing meals, and enjoy the process of cooking and eating in a way that supports your well-being.

Printed in Great Britain
by Amazon